HELPING PEC

Educational theory and practice are historically influenced by the view of behavioral psychologists that learning is synonymous with behavior change. *Helping People Learn* argues for the practical importance of an alternate view: that learning is synonymous with a change in the meaning of experience. Based on the foundations of cognitive psychology and constructivist epistemology, this book presents a science of education that can guide the development of successful and meaningful educational programs. It serves as a sequel to the best-selling *Learning How to Learn* and includes ideas developed through the author's research and training programs conducted over the past thirty years. It emphasizes the power of the knowledge representation tool "concept maps," designed to facilitate meaningful learning and creativity. This book capitalizes on the advances in technology and is of interest to students, professionals, and researchers in educational psychology and learning theory.

JOSEPH D. NOVAK is Senior Research Scientist Emeritus at the Florida Institute for Human and Machine Cognition (IHMC) and Professor Emeritus at Cornell University. He is the author or contributing author of 40 books and more than 150 research papers. He has made significant contributions in educational psychology and science education.

HELPING PEOPLE LEARN

JOSEPH D. NOVAK

*Cornell University and Florida Institute for Human
and Machine Cognition*

CAMBRIDGE
UNIVERSITY PRESS

CAMBRIDGE
UNIVERSITY PRESS

University Printing House, Cambridge CB2 8BS, United Kingdom

One Liberty Plaza, 20th Floor, New York, NY 10006, USA

477 Williamstown Road, Port Melbourne, VIC 3207, Australia

314–321, 3rd Floor, Plot 3, Splendor Forum, Jasola District Centre, New Delhi – 110025, India

103 Penang Road, #05–06/07, Visioncrest Commercial, Singapore 238467

Cambridge University Press is part of the University of Cambridge.

It furthers the University's mission by disseminating knowledge in the pursuit of
education, learning, and research at the highest international levels of excellence.

www.cambridge.org
Information on this title: www.cambridge.org/9781108470896
DOI: 10.1017/9781108625982

First published 2022

A catalogue record for this publication is available from the British Library.

Library of Congress Cataloging-in-Publication Data
NAMES: Novak, Joseph D. (Joseph Donald), author.
TITLE: Helping people learn / Joseph D. Novak, Cornell University and Florida Institute for Human
and Machine Cognition.
DESCRIPTION: New York, NY : Cambridge University Press, [2022] | Includes bibliographical
references and index.
IDENTIFIERS: LCCN 2022012588 | ISBN 9781108470896 (hardback) | ISBN 9781108456838
(paperback)
SUBJECTS: LCSH: Learning, Psychology of. | Education–Philosophy. | Educational psychology.
| Climatic changes–Social aspects. | BISAC: PSYCHOLOGY / General
CLASSIFICATION: LCC LB1060 .N676 2022 | DDC 370.15/23–dc23/eng/20220503
LC record available at https://lccn.loc.gov/2022012588

ISBN 978-1-108-47089-6 Hardback
ISBN 978-1-108-45683-8 Paperback

Contents

Figures

Preface

In some ways, this book had its origins in 1979–1980. In a conversation with Professor Joel Mintzes at the University of North Carolina – Wilmington, in 1980, I mentioned that I was looking for a good place to spend my next sabbatical leave in the coming academic year working on a new book.

Joel was also the first Ph.D. student of Darryl Murray, my first Ph.D. student at Purdue University, so he was both familiar with my work and interested in collaborating with me professionally. Sabbatical leave arrangements were made, and we spent several months of the 1980–1981 academic year in an ocean front condominium we owned on Carolina Beach. The sabbatical leave arrangements proved to be helpful in other ways, and Joel Mintzes and I became lifelong associates.

I used copies of the first draft of the text in my Learning to Learn course that I first introduced in 1978 at Cornell University. It was later published by Cambridge University Press in 1984, and subsequently in several other languages. The book drew heavily on my experiences with teaching that course. It also drew on the theoretical foundations I had presented in my 1977 book, *A Theory of Education* (Novak, 1977a). The latter book, published by Cornell University Press, drew upon work done by my research teams and visiting professors, as well as a graduate course I called "Theory and Method of Education." I continued to teach both of these courses until 1995 when I retired from my position at Cornell University. I had invited my colleague, D. Bob Gowin, to co-author *Learning How to Learn*, and we continued our collaboration until his retirement in 1993.

My wife, Joan, had open heart surgery in January, 1994, and she thought she would do better spending winters in an area that is warm, flat, and at sea level. I had begun doing some consulting work with Procter & Gamble in Cincinnati, Ohio, and I could continue this work from any location in the country. I thought the theory, principles, and tools we had developed could also be employed successfully in other organizational settings.

I thought that retirement from Cornell University could provide opportunities to work in many other organizational settings to help people learn. As you will see in this book, this aspiration proved to be very successful.

As I was considering possible universities for my 1987–1988 sabbatical leave, I had a chance conversation with a former Ph.D. student from Cornell University, Bruce Dunn, a professor in the Psychology Department at the University of West Florida (UWF). Bruce suggested that funding might be available for me if I were to spend my sabbatical at his university. Bruce had assembled electroencephalographic (EEG) equipment to study brain activity. I thought it would be interesting to see how EEG patterns differed when subjects were working with different types of concept maps. UWF is about twenty miles from Pensacola Beach, a beautiful Gulf Coast place to live and work for the academic year, and I chose to accept the UWF position of Visiting Research Professor.

Kenneth Ford, a close friend of Bruce Dunn, joined the faculty of Computer Science in the fall of 1988. We soon became acquainted, and Ken became intrigued with the possibility of using concept maps to characterize expert knowledge, one of the difficult problems in the field of artificial intelligence. *Concept maps* are a knowledge representation and learning tool we developed in my research program at Cornell University in the early 1970s. A local cardiologist, Dr. Roberts, had developed a machine for diagnosing coronary defects. The problem was that he had difficulty training other cardiologists to use his equipment. Ken formed a team to concept map Dr. Roberts' diagnostic ideas and strategies. The training program developed using these concept maps proved to be very successful. This led to contracts with all branches of the military, NASA, NSA, and a number of other organizations. Ken had developed the Institute for Human and Machine Cognition (IHMC) to serve as the administrative unit for all of these projects.

The 1980s saw the explosive development of the personal computer. Ken saw the need for high-quality software to make it easier to construct and utilize concept maps in a wide variety of applications. In 1990 Ken brought in a longtime friend, Professor Alberto Cañas, to lead the team to develop what became known as CmapTools software. I am deeply indebted to Alberto and his teams for creating this wonderful software, now used all over the world. This process is described in Chapter 2 of this book. The software is available to anyone at no cost at: http://cmap.ihmc.us/.

When the World Wide Web was developed in the later 1990s and early 2000s, IHMC became a leader in developing software that would facilitate the use of information from the World Wide Web. CmapTools provided for gathering digital resources from the Internet, or any other source, and moving these into the files for concept maps, making these essentially a knowledge portfolio. This opened up many new opportunities for the use of this tool in helping people in all organizations gather, organize, and use creatively this wealth of information.

As an undergraduate student at the University of Minnesota, I was struck by the contrast between the validity of the knowledge presented in the science courses that I had taken and the unsupported claims so often made in education courses. The sciences presented a body of knowledge comprising concepts, principles, and theories that explain how and why things in the universe behave as they do. There was almost nothing comparable to this in the courses I took in education. Nevertheless, education is a phenomenon conducted by people and there is no inherent reason why it could not also be guided by a body of concepts, principles, and theories. I devoted a good bit of my time and energies to the goal of developing a science of education. Although I do not present the details of this journey in this book, I do sketch some of the early battles and later successes in the development of my theory of education.

Throughout my public school years and most of my undergraduate years at the University of Minnesota, I found schooling to be reading information in the book, or recording information from lectures to be memorized, then taking objective true–false or multiple-choice tests that required little more than recall of information – and then forgetting almost everything in six weeks! Unfortunately, the latter is essentially what most students are doing in most schools. I was fortunate to have a few school teachers and professors whom I remember fondly as persons who challenged me to think. But now we are beginning to see some colleges and universities applying what we have learned about human learning and problem-solving, encouraging modified instructional programs and alternative evaluation programs. I present some of these new approaches in the last two chapters of this book.

The memorize-test-forget kind of education described in the last paragraph is inherently fraudulent. The consequence of this is that students who experience such education fail to become creative problem-solvers in whatever roles they take as adults. It is probably also one reason why only about 40 percent of young adults accept the responsibility to vote in national elections. With the challenges the peoples of the world face with climate change, we are in a race with time to improve schooling at all levels in all countries. We are almost certain to see massive deaths and property destruction on a scale that makes the Covid-19 pandemic a small incident by comparison. In Chapters 4 and 5, I discuss some of the possible changes we may see in school education in general and in medical education more specifically. With the right leadership,

I believe it will be possible to achieve the kinds of changes in educational programs that are needed as well as other necessary changes in social institutions. Finding ways to deal with the Covid-19 virus catalyzes some creative innovations in education and in the workplace.

Throughout my career I have been blessed with the love, support, and thoughtful counsel of my wife, Joan. My three children have been a joy to us, and I have learned much from them. I have been fortunate to have had many outstanding students and visiting professors, many of whom continue to advance programs we had initiated together. It was my good fortune to have strong, supportive administrative leadership in all of my positions, and especially at Cornell University.

In 1990, Alberto Cañas joined the institute as Associate Director, and the Florida Institute for Human and Machine Cognition was fully underway. As noted earlier Alberto led a team of workers to develop the outstanding software suite CmapTools that will be described more fully in Chapter 2. The institute expanded its operations and became an independent agency under the title of the Florida Institute for Human and Machine Cognition.

From the 1990s onward, it was my pleasure to work with a number of members of IHMC to solve various problems, as will be described in the chapters of this book. In addition to the strong support and involvement of Kenneth Ford and Alberto Cañas, a number of other colleagues have assisted me in my work and in the preparation of this book. These include Alan Ordway, an able master of computers and computer software, always available to answer a question when problems would arise. Julie Sheppard, Administrative Assistant to Kenneth Ford, has assisted in various tasks including provision of permissions for some of the materials included. Several of the staff members have helped develop materials included in the book including Roger Carp, William Howel, and Robert Hoffman. When Joan and I moved to the Sheraton Senior Living Residence in Lakewood Ranch, Florida, it was my good fortune to obtain the volunteer services of Dee Humphreys in typing the many revisions and the final manuscript for the book. David Tangren has also assisted me in some of the final tasks associated with the completion of the manuscript and the preparation of materials for final submission. To all of these people, I am deeply indebted for their voluntary assistance. Finally, I wish to thank my wife, Joan who has dealt with many hours of isolation as I have worked on the manuscript and required silent study. In so many ways Joan has been for me the wind beneath my wings as well as a loving companion.

CHAPTER I

Developing the Foundations to Help People Learn

Why Young Children Learn So Quickly

If you have had the experience of interacting with a child between the ages of one and four, you have witnessed how quickly these children acquire the names for objects and events they are experiencing. They also demonstrate their ability to pronounce these names, albeit their pronunciation may not be perfect at first. Usually, mommy and daddy are among the first words learned, but a dog's name or the name of a favorite toy might also be learned very early. The name of a favorite food or drink may appear very early. Children add about ten to twenty new words a week between the ages of 18 to 24 months. By age four the average child can use about 4,000 words correctly. Most adults know the meanings of 20,000 to 35,000 words.

The most difficult thing any person will have to learn in their lifetime is to speak and understand the language. And yet, all normal children do this by age four! Why then do so many children have trouble learning in school when they were so successful as young children? This book will help to answer this question and to provide some solutions to this problem. We will also discuss what we can do to help people learn in any setting, from the classroom to the job setting to the research laboratory.

In my work as an educator and researcher for the past sixty plus years, I have found that it is critically important for teachers and learners to understand that most words are names for concepts. We define a concept as a perceived regularity or pattern in events or objects, or records of events or objects, designated by a word or symbol. When children learn the meaning of most new words, they are really learning the meaning of concepts. They are learning what pattern or regularity they are for. Concepts are the building blocks of knowledge in every domain of knowledge.

When young children acquire names for concepts, they are almost always observing the events or objects to which the word label is being applied. They are seeing and experiencing things such as dogs, or liquids, birds, or trees. Or they may be experiencing events such as running, fishing, cooking, or bathing. These concept labels have *meaning* for the children. They are engaged in *meaningful learning*. By contrast, so much of school learning involves rote memorization of definitions of words or statements for which the child has no direct experience. We label this kind of learning *rote learning*, and this kind of learning can lead to many kinds of educational problems. A continuing theme in this book will be that we must find better ways to enhance and facilitate meaningful learning in schools or work settings, and to minimize as much as possible engaging people in rote learning.

New concepts are created by creative people who observe a new pattern or regularity in some specific kind of thing or event. They describe and define this regularity and give it a name. For example, I am typing this book on a laptop computer. These had not been invented when I was a student.

Macnamara (1982) saw in his studies of how children acquire "names for things" that either the perception of a regularity or the name (word) for a regularity may come first, but facility in proper use of the word requires that both the word label and its associated meaning be integrated. Since meaning is always context-dependent, the meaning of a concept label will always have some idiosyncratic elements, for no two people experience an identical sequence of events (contexts) in which a given concept label is applied. Whorf (1956) was one of the first and most prominent researchers to recognize that the cultural context in which a person lives shapes the meaning of that person's concepts. (Novak, 2010, p. 43).

Important as it is to understand the meaning of concepts in any domain of knowledge, learning a set of concept names does not lead to an understanding of the meaning of these concepts. We also must learn valid propositions that incorporate these concepts. *Propositions* are two or more concepts connected with linking words to form a meaningful statement. Thus, we really never learn the meaning of a concept in isolation but, rather, through learning sets of propositions that include that concept. So, the young child learns that sky is blue, water is wet, dogs can bark, etcetera, etcetera.

We might compare the world of language with the world of chemistry. The universe is made up of about 100 kinds of atoms or elements. Two or more atoms may combine to form a molecule. The possible combinations of atoms are essentially infinite, and there is no end to the number of new molecules a chemist may invent. Similarly, there are just twenty-six letters in the English language, and words are made up of one or more letters. When creative people see or invent some new pattern or regularity, they make up a word to label this new concept. Consider for a moment all the new words invented to describe new patterns in objects and events in the digital world.

So, the fundamental challenge we face in helping people learn in any domain of knowledge is to help people build an understanding of the key concepts and propositions of that discipline. We also want to help them to understand how new knowledge can be created in that discipline. There has been so much written about how to help people learn that we also need to sort out which ideas are valid and may be powerful, and which ideas are of little value or just plain wrong. For me, this has been a lifelong journey – and the journey will continue as long as I am able to pursue it. We are continuing to find better ways to help people learn. And new technologies are opening up new possibilities that we need to consider.

We are usually at our best in new learning when we are also engaged in some physical activity. If we are progressing well with our learning, we also experience strong positive feelings. Recall your experience when you figured out how something works or a winning strategy for a game. Thinking, feeling, and acting are all integrated in a positive way in any successful learning experience.

Figure 1.1 The author's three children, Barbara (7), William (6), Joseph (8), 1965. Raising children was a joy for me; they also taught me so much!

I have discussed in some detail in my biography three things that have been helpful in my search for understanding how people learn and how to facilitate learning.[1] First, my experiences as a parent raising three children have not only been a great joy but have helped me discern those ideas I was taught that made sense from those perspectives that did not. Second, my wife for more than six decades has been both a constant supporter and the best critic of my work. Third, as a child, my dad played a very important role in building my confidence. He insisted that his son Joe was capable of doing anything he sought to do. I will also indicate in this book instances where these people helped me discern sense from nonsense – and there is much of the latter in the literature!

Can Education Become a Science?

I majored in science as an undergraduate and also completed classes and intern teaching to become a certified science teacher. As a graduate student, I was a research and teaching assistant in the Botany Department at the University of Minnesota. I also completed the requirements for a Ph.D. degree in Science Education. I was fascinated by the methods scientists used to create new knowledge and the important role that theories play in the advance of science. By contrast, I learned of no real theories or major principles that could guide educational practice and knowledge creation in education that would lead to better educational practices. It was my conviction that human learning and educational practices could be considered as belonging to the class of animal behavior and therefore should be amenable to the same kinds of tools and theory building that have been so successful in the sciences. I came to believe that if education were ever to become a science, it must be based on a valid theory of learning. I was convinced that behavioral psychology was not viable as a theory to guide education and educational research.

Throughout my undergraduate and graduate education at the University of Minnesota from 1948 to 1957, the only theory of learning I was taught was behavioral psychology. The fundamental idea of behavioral psychology is that since we cannot observe directly what is occurring in the brain, we must study only the manifest behaviors of animals and humans. We cannot therefore attempt to speculate on what is going on in their brains. Furthermore, behavioral psychology largely ignores the important role that feelings play in everything that people choose to do.

---

[1] This biography is available at no cost at: www.ihmc.us/joseph.

Any theory that ignored the role of feelings, in my view, was quite simply inadequate at best and possibly dead wrong!

In the sciences, many kinds of studies deal with phenomena that we cannot observe directly, but only through the use of instruments. For example, almost everything we know about the structure and function of atoms is derived through observations with instruments. So, concepts in this field are created primarily from patterns in records we make, not from observing events and objects with our own eyes. From my perspective, behavioral psychology simply did not make sense as a theoretical model, nor did I think it was a viable theory to guide research on human learning. One lesson I learned from my dad's teaching was that if something just does not make sense, it is probably wrong. For a few years, I and my graduate students searched for a better theory of human learning to guide our work.

Learning to Understand and to Implement Ausubel's Assimilation Theory of Learning

My first job was in the Biology Department at Kansas State Teachers College. I taught undergraduate and graduate biology courses and supervised a small group of master's degree students interested in research on biology teaching and learning. In 1959, I accepted a joint position as Assistant Professor in the Biology and Education Departments at Purdue University. My primary responsibilities were to build a nationally recognized program for training biology teachers and to conduct research with MS and Ph.D. graduate students interested in improving biology education. I inherited a few Ph.D. students from my predecessor who held this position before he was killed in an automobile accident. Within two years, I had built a team with eight–ten Ph.D. students.

Not only was behavioral psychology the dominant theory for learning during my school years, but it remained the dominant theory until the late 1980s. I saw no value in behavioral psychology as a theory of learning for a science education research program. I and my team of graduate students were delighted when we learned about David Ausubel's Assimilation Theory of Learning first published as a journal article in 1962, and as a book in 1963. So, beginning in 1963, we finally had a theory of learning that made sense to us! Much of the success my students and I achieved in coming to understand human learning and finding new ways to facilitate such learning derived from rejecting behavioral psychology and embracing Ausubel's new Assimilation Theory of Learning.

Although Ausubel's learning theory contained only seven major principles, it was not easy to understand, since each of the principles is closely connected with the meanings of the other six principles. I discussed earlier in this chapter the differences between rote learning and meaningful learning. Ausubel has written more precisely than any other cognitive psychologist I have studied. His theory includes the important differences that occur when a learner acquires information by meaningful learning as contrasted to learning by rote memorization. His theory includes the principle of *subsumption* that occurs in meaningful learning when new examples of concepts are *subsumed* and integrated into a *relevant* existing, more general concept. For example, this is the case when a child learns that another kind of animal they never saw before is also a member of the dog family. Repeated subsumption of new instances or examples of a concept lead to a refinement and enhancement over time of this subsuming concept. Ausubel called this process *progressive differentiation.* The subsuming concept becomes more complex and inclusive, but also more explicit and more precisely understood. A young child might confuse a cat as another kind of dog. But she/he will soon differentiate these kinds of animals and recognize that while they can both be *pets* (another concept), they are distinctly different. Even as a young child, these kinds of subsumptions and progressive differentiations take place effectively with all normal children.

As a child's learning progresses, she/he may learn that some people have parrots or canaries as pets, and maybe hamsters and white rats. A new superordinate concept of household pet may be forming, perhaps including cold-blooded animals such as turtles, fish, and snakes. Over time, some details of these expanded concepts may be forgotten in the process Ausubel called *obliterative subsumption.* There is a difference between obliterative subsumption that may occur after meaningful learning and *forgetting* that occurs after rote learning. In the case of obliterative subsumption of concept details, the contributions that obliteratively subsumed concepts had made to the meaning of the superordinate concept largely remain and these can be quickly relearned. No such cognitive benefit occurs in the *forgetting* that occurs after rote learning. Figure 1.2 summarizes these seven Quasiabelian learning principles, shown in shaded ovals.

One way to move toward better understanding of these principles of learning is to try placing examples of concepts of objects or events that interest you as specific examples of each principle. For example, you might use cars as another example, or events such as parties or travel.

When we memorize new information, that is when we learn by rote, that information can be stored almost anywhere in our frontal cortex (see

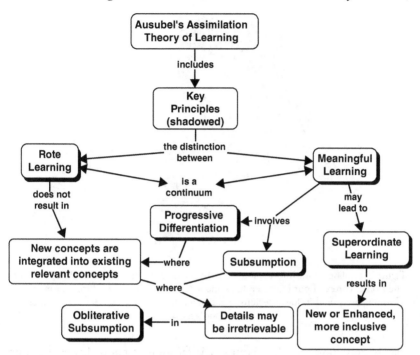

Figure 1.2   A concept map showing the relationship of key principles in Ausubel's Assimilation Theory of Learning. The key ideas in Ausubel's theory are shown in the shaded concept cells of the map.

Figure 1.3). When we learn information meaningfully, this new information becomes integrated with related concepts and propositions stored in our cortex. Ausubel called this a subsumption process. When this occurs, both the original anchoring concept and the added subsumed concept are modified in a positive way. Ausubel describes this as assimilating new knowledge into existing relevant concepts. Thus, his theory of learning is often called Ausubel's Assimilation Theory of Learning. For the young child, almost all learning takes place when they are interacting with objects or events and thus most of their learning is meaningful. By contrast, so much of school learning involves memorization or rote learning of information that has few or no ties to the real world of objects and events already known by the learner.

I recall when my son Joe was about two years old and we were driving in the countryside. My son saw a cow in a field that we passed and he shouted out: "doggy, doggy." I said no – it is really a cow that is much bigger than a

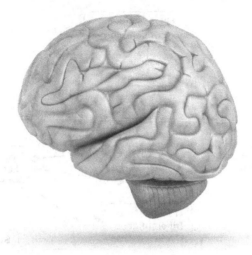

Figure 1.3   The brain. Information we learn is stored in the outer convoluted folds of the frontal cortex of our brain. Feelings and actions, we experience during meaningful learning are stored in lower regions of the brain, but all are connected by nerve cells and blood vessels.

dog. It only looks smaller because it is far away. I guess this explanation made sense to my son; he never made this mistake again – and he assimilated a new idea about dogs and other animals that might look like dogs when viewed from a distance. The idea that things viewed some distance away look smaller than they really are is a pretty powerful concept, and we have observed this often in our work with children.

From 1963 to this day, Ausubel's Assimilation Theory of Learning has been useful to me and my research groups and to my students. As our work progressed, it became increasingly evident that meaningful learning was not a simple alternative to rote learning. Since meaningful learning requires that the learner must make the effort to integrate new concepts and propositions with relevant concepts and propositions she/he already knows, the quality of meaningful learning is dependent on both the quality of relevant concepts and propositions the learner holds and also the degree to which the learner makes an effort to integrate new knowledge into her/ his existing relevant knowledge. Both of these aspects can vary greatly from learner to learner and for different learning tasks. Sitting and listening to a lecture is a very poor way to engage in a high level of meaningful learning. Actively working with and discussing with a team of students a new idea or a new way of doing something can be a great way to engage in high levels of meaningful learning. Throughout this book I shall try to illustrate that working and thinking with others is a great way to help people learn.

When I began college at the University of Minnesota in 1948, one thing I had hoped to learn was how people learn and create new things. From my readings, it was clear that people who create new things and new ideas are intelligent, and they work very hard. The book that I read in 1949 that had perhaps the most important influence on my thinking was James Conant's, *On Understanding Science*. Conant argued that what makes advances in the sciences is that people invent new conceptual schemes, and then they work to refine, modify, and improve these schemes. Sometimes they see that a given conceptual scheme begins to have too many problems or inconsistencies, and then comes the challenge to create a new, better scheme. Conant also suggested that the process goes on forever, and we will never invent the perfectly correct conceptual scheme!

As a college freshman, I did not know at the time that Conant's ideas were far from the mainstream of the thinking of philosophers and psychologists. Overwhelmingly in these fields, the popular belief was that through careful observations and experimentation, we can eventually establish laws, and these laws will endure forever. These kinds of thinkers were called positivists or logical positivists. The University of Minnesota was the international center for logical positivism. I did a graduate philosophy course with one of the world leaders, Professor Herbert Feigl. Professor Feigl and I had several friendly debates in his office – which he easily won by sheer years of professing. Nevertheless, I thought the kind of philosophy I was searching for would be better than logical positivism.

All the psychology courses I took at Minnesota were based on behavioral psychology, and this psychology was tightly wedded to positivist thinking. For various reasons, I thought that the logical positivists and the behavioral psychologists were just plain wrong in their assumptions, their methodologies, and their thinking! The confidence my dad helped to build in me as a child gave me the guts to insist that the behaviorists and the positivists were just plain wrong and people like Conant in philosophy of science and Ausubel in psychology were on the right track. Be certain of this, my views were far from the mainstream in the 1950s through the 1970s. Fortunately, the tide of thinking had turned in my direction by the mid-1980s. The changes in thinking in psychology in the 1970s and 1980s became what some call the "cognitive psychology revolution," bringing the thinking in psychology much more in line with Ausubel's 1963 ideas.

There were other scholars who were critical of behavioral psychology as early as the 1920s. I simply was not exposed to any of their work in my psychology courses at Minnesota. Piaget had published several books on children's cognitive development in the 1920s through the 1970s. Noam Chomsky had published his critique of behaviorism and empiricist episte-mology in 1959. In 1960, Jerome Bruner and George Miller founded the Harvard Center for Cognitive Studies, the first formal institution commit-ted to cognitive psychology. In 1967, Ulrick Neisser published his book, *Cognitive Psychology*, and this defined cognitive psychology for decades to come.

Almost simultaneously, the thinking about the nature of knowledge and knowledge creation began to shift toward constructivist views, more similar to Conant than to Feigl and other positivist's ideas. The current views are congruent with the kind of thinking my students and I had been using since the early 1960s. I have describe my intellectual journey up to my current work in a book that can be downloaded and read at: www .ihmc.us/joseph-novak/.

In 1977, David Ausubel invited me to collaborate on a revision of his 1968 book, *Educational Psychology: A Cognitive View*. My job was to revise the chapters dealing with Ausubel's Assimilation Theory of Learning, and some other sections of the book. In the course of working on these revisions, I got to know Ausubel very well and we had numerous conver-sations about his theoretical ideas and possible modifications. The revised second edition was published in 1978. (Ausubel, Novak, and Hanesian, 1978). The sale of the English edition was dropped by the publishers (Holt, Rinehart, and Winston) after five years when annual sales of the book dropped below their required level, but the Spanish translation published by Editorial Trills in Mexico continues to sell today. The international rise of cognitive psychology was yet to come. My colleague, Ulrich Neisser, published his *Cognitive Psychology* in 1967, and this became a classic in the field, but this book did not come to my attention until ten or twelve years later. Anderson's 1983 book became very popular as cognitive psychology began to dominate the field. Ausubel regarded the latter book and similar books as neo-behaviorist, and I saw them as failing to shed the positivistic views of behavioral psychology. The complex interrelationships of the ideas in Ausubel's Assimilation Theory of Learning did not compete well with some of the other books on cognitive psychology mentioned above and the still widely popular behavioral psychology books published in the 1970s and 1980s.

Based on research done by my research teams, and my teaching expe-riences presenting these ideas to others, I argued that rote learning and meaningful learning should not be viewed as discrete forms of learning, but rather as two ends of a continuum, as noted earlier in this chapter. I observed that when learners first began learning about a new domain of knowledge, their understanding of key concepts in that domain was relatively limited and they had little or no understanding of how concepts in that domain were related to each other. As learners gained expertise in a domain of knowledge, they began to see and understand many more connections between concepts in that domain, thus building a much greater understanding of all these interrelated concepts. The integration of new concepts and propositions related to this domain becomes more richly integrated. As this integration of new concepts related to this domain became more interconnected, each concept and proposition had deeper meaning for these learners. Marton and Säljö (1976a, 1976b) have used the label deep learning as contrasted to surface learning to describe the differences we have referred to as meaningful in contrast to rote learning. There are similarities in their work to the ideas we were developing.

I argued further that what I and my students observed in our research was that those individuals who came to them with new ideas, that is new related concepts and propositions, were essentially doing very high levels of meaningful learning. This suggested that we could represent this as show-ing that creative learning was best viewed as part of a learning continuum but at very high levels of meaningful learning. After we developed the concept mapping tool, to be discussed later in this chapter, it was very easy to see explicit examples of students or researchers progressing in the quality and extent of their meaningful learning for a given domain of knowledge.

Although Ausubel initially did not support the view that rote learning and meaningful learning are best seen as two ends of a continuum, he did accept this idea in his later writing (Ausubel, 2000). I also argued in later years that creativity can be viewed as a very high level of meaningful learning. Therefore, if we wish to encourage individuals to think creatively, we must help them become powerful meaningful learners. These ideas are illustrated in Figure 1.4.

While verbal learning takes place in the cortex of the brain, this region is richly connected with other areas of the brain. Some lower regions of the brain include areas that primarily store visual informa-tion, coordinate muscle activity and the feelings experienced when learning or doing anything, as well as regions involved in autonomous activities such as breathing and digestion. To become a skilled athlete or an accomplished musician requires building connections between the frontal cortex and many other regions of the brain. This is one reason it

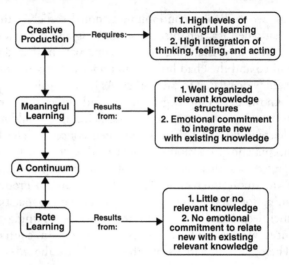

Figure 1.4   Rote and meaningful learning may be viewed as two ends of a continuum,
and creativity is seen as resulting from very high levels of meaningful learning.
This figure will be referred to frequently, so it might be helpful to print a
copy of this figure and post it in your study.

takes years to become a skilled musician or an accomplished artist or
athlete. It is truly remarkable how well the human body integrates all of
our thinking, feeling and acting in ways that allow humans to do such
remarkable things.

Another important feature of meaningful learning is that it usually
involves some form of action on the part of the learner and these actions
are accompanied by feelings, either positive or negative, that occur during
the actions. Thus, in meaningful learning we not only have new concepts
and propositions integrated with relevant existing concepts and propositions, we also have feelings and actions integrated into the developing
concept and propositional framework. This integration of thinking, feeling
and acting during meaningful learning confers enhanced retention and
future usability of these concepts and propositions.

So, the short answer to the question: What makes the learning of young
children so effective is: most of their learning occurs in settings where they
are integrating their thinking, feeling, and acting, while dealing with real
events or objects. They are engaged with the objects and events labeled by
the words they are learning and experiencing the connections of these
words in ways that make sense to them. The result is that young children
are highly effective meaningful learners. What we seek to do in this book is

to illustrate how we can help learners of any age become more effective meaningful learners, just as they were in preschool years. We shall also explore how new learning tools and ideas can enhance learning effectiveness at any age and in any domain of knowledge.

How Can We Encourage and Facilitate Meaningful Learning?

In the course of my research programs, first at Purdue University from 1959 to 1967 and then at Cornell University from 1967 to 1998, my teams conducted a number of research projects that dealt with children's and adult's learning. Almost all of these studies were done in real-world classrooms or other real-world settings for learning. Throughout this book we will show how some of these research projects led to new ways to help people learn.

One of my research projects involved young children learning basic science concepts with the aid of Audio-tutorial (A-T) instruction. A-T tutorial instruction was first developed at Purdue University with Professor Postlethwait with his Introductory Botany course.[2] I adapted A-T instruction to teach basic science concepts to grade 1 and grade 2 children while on sabbatical leave at Harvard University in 1965–1966. Figure 1.5 shows a seven-year-old child learning about the conversion of electrical energy to other forms of energy. Most of the lessons in our A-T program were based on an elementary science series that I had written, published in 1966. I will say more about this project in later chapters.

We designed a group of A-T science lessons in the 1960s in order to teach basic science concepts to children in primary grades. Very few elementary school teachers have the science knowledge, or the materials needed, to teach about the nature of matter and energy, necessary requirements for living things to live, etc. The conventional wisdom, based in part on Jean Piaget's work with children, was that children cannot begin to understand these abstract concepts of science until age thirteen or older. My experiences with my three children, and some limited research with primary school children, indicated that this was not true, and one objective of our study was to prove this. Most important was our goal to demonstrate an effective way to bring high-quality science instruction into elementary schools (Hibbard and Novak, 1975).

---

[2] See Postlethwait, Novak, and Murray, 1964; 1972.

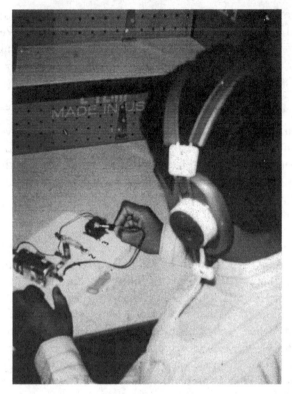

Figure 1.5   A grade 2 child experimenting with converting electric energy from a battery into heat, light, and motion in apparatus developed in an A-T program.

The Invention of the Concept Map as a Knowledge Representation Tool

When we interviewed and talked with the children after instruction, it was obvious that the children were beginning to acquire an understanding of the concepts we were teaching. The problem was that we needed a better assessment strategy to demonstrate convincingly that the children were developing a genuine understanding of the concepts and propositions we were teaching. My research team turned to the theoretical foundations in Ausubel's learning theory and constructivist ideas about how humans construct new knowledge. We came up with these basic ideas to guide our search for better evaluation tools:

1. All knowledge is composed of concepts linked to form meaningful statements or propositions.
2. In meaningful learning, knowledge is stored hierarchically, with the more general and inclusive concepts at the top and the more specific concepts at lower levels of a knowledge structure.
3. As children learn more about any domain of knowledge, they should build more elaborate, more accurate knowledge structures for that domain.

The solution to our assessment problem did not occur in one sudden insight. My research team struggled with this problem for a few years in the early 1970s. We tried studying individual statements or propositions made in the interviews with the children. We made lists of these propositions given by children and recorded in our interview transcripts.

We finally settled on building a hierarchy of concepts and propositions starting with the most general, most inclusive concepts in a given interview and working on down to the most specific, least inclusive concepts. We also added linking words connecting the concepts to form propositions, recording these just as they were given by the children in our interviews.

Organizing the concepts in the children's statements in our interviews in this way gave us what we called a *concept map*. The latter approach proved to be the most useful, most explicit way to illustrate what a child had learned on a given topic. This approach was also the most congruent with our theoretical foundations. Figures 1.6 and 1.7 show concept maps drawn from interviews with Cindy, one of the students in our research study. Originally, the maps were dawn using pens or pencils, but I no longer have these maps in my files. After we developed computer software to make it easy to draw concept maps, all of our concept maps were done using this software. I discuss the development of this software in the next chapter.

One of our interviews with Cindy was done near the end of grade 2, after two years of A-T science instruction. This concept map shows that Cindy had begun to understand some basic concepts about the structure of matter, although some of her ideas are faulty, or she could not recall the correct label for the concepts. She uses the label "little bits" and "very tiny specks" rather than atoms or molecules. This is a common observation we see with students of all ages. She also has the faulty idea that the little bits are "squeezable." One of the A-T lessons used small balloons to illustrate that the air the subject blew into the balloon took up space, but remained

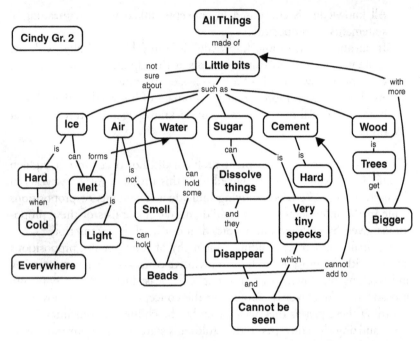

Figure 1.6 A concept map prepared by one of the author's graduate students from the transcript of an interview with Cindy in grade 2, following two years of A-T instruction in science. She is beginning to understand the concepts of atoms and molecules but has more to learn, including the scientific name for "small bits."

squeezable, unlike a balloon filled with water. It is quite common to observe in interviews with individuals of any age that they confer the properties of the whole thing they are observing to the particles that make up the whole thing. Cindy has obviously acquired some understanding of the idea that the things we see are made up of tiny particles. This is a good beginning for later learning about atoms and molecules that are the building blocks of all matter.

Owing to limited funding, my research team could not continue the A-T science instruction in grades 3 to 6, as we had originally planned to do. I described my struggles to obtain funding for this project in my biography, cited footnote 1. My team did manage to do follow-up interviews with samples of the original students in the study in grades 7, 10, and 12. We observed some gains in understanding of basic science concepts, as a result of enrollment in conventional junior and senior high science courses. However, there were striking differences in performance

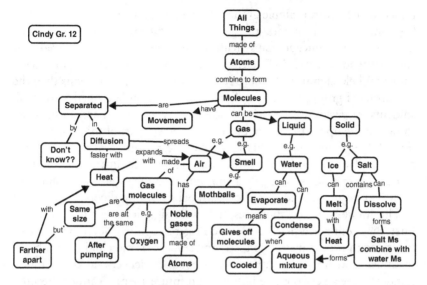

Figure 1.7   A concept map prepared from an interview with Cindy near the end of grade 12. It shows that Cindy has made good progress in understanding the nature of matter.

between the children who had the A-T lessons in grades 1 and 2 and a similar sample of students who did not have these lessons.

My research team made a concerted effort to interview all the original students who participated in the study who were still in Ithaca schools in grade 12. The concept map in Figure 1.7 was drawn from the transcript of an interview with Cindy toward the end of grade 12. Compare the ideas in this map with those shown above in her map in grade 2 and you can see that Cindy did indeed learn much more about the nature of matter as she progressed through her school years.

My research team found that the children who received the early A-T lessons in grades 1 and 2 very significantly outperformed their schoolmates who did not receive these early science lessons. These results supported Ausubel's learning theory that says if children begin to form valid anchoring concepts in early years, this will advantage them in all future learning of related concepts in later years. We see evidence of this in Cindy's grade 12 concept map.

By the time the students in our study reached grade 12, there were only 38 students from the original instructed sample still enrolled in Ithaca schools. There were seventeen students still available from the uninstructed control sample group who had no A-T lessons. All these had been interviewed in grades 2, 7, 10, and 12 by my research teams. The analysis of the concept maps made from these interviews showed that children who received A-T science lessons in grades 1 and 2 (instructed students) held significantly more *valid* concepts and propositions than the uninstructed group, and this difference increased in later grades when all students received regular school science instruction. These results are shown in the upper part of Figure 1.8. The lower part of this figure shows that the A-T instructed children held fewer *invalid* notions and the number of these declined with additional science instruction in later grades. The results were highly significant, and they were consistent with what had been expected, based on Ausubel's learning theory.[3]

The findings of the above research were significant for three reasons. First, they confirmed that, contrary to Piaget's cognitive development stage theory, with proper instruction, six- and seven-year-old children can begin to understand important abstract concepts of science, and these understanding have a very positive influence on future science learning. Second, the results support Ausubel's Assimilation Theory of Learning that predicts that when given high-quality, meaningful instruction in science in early grades, children will begin to form subsumers or anchoring concepts that will facilitate later science learning and diminish the formation of invalid ideas or misconceptions. Third, the study showed that concept maps can be a very useful evaluation tool for cognitive learning (see Novak, 2004).

I wish I could show you similar results from similar research. However, I have found no other study that followed the cognitive development of the *same children* in a specific subject matter area through twelve years of schooling. Having struggled with the funding and logistical problems we experienced, it is easy to understand why this is the case. Later researchers have shown that A-T instruction can be effective. Kulik, Kulik, and Cohen (1979) published a meta-analysis of research on the use of A-T methods, showing the general superior effectiveness of this teaching strategy.

When the Cognitive Psychology Revolution occurred in the late 1980s and beyond, researchers such as Donaldson (1978), Chi (1983), and many others began to do research that supported the kind of research results our team had found, albeit with studies of much shorter durations. The Cornell University program to help people learn had a twenty-year head start as a result of our early embrace of a cognitive learning theory and with practice in applying the ideas to improve student's learning.

---

[3] See Novak and Musonda, 1991, and Novak, 2004.

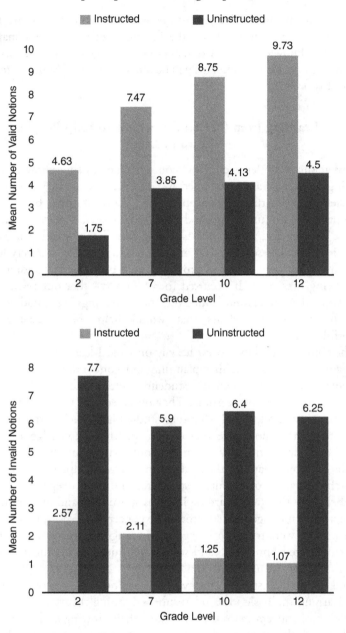

Figure 1.8   Grade levels. This figure shows that students who had A-T science lessons in grades 1 and 2 (instructed) held substantially more valid science notions in high school (top of the figure), and far fewer invalid notions (misconceptions) in high school grades (lower part of the figure). (See Novak, 2004.)

Important as the twelve-year study was for debunking some myths about children's learning, it was the invention of the concept map tool to represent knowledge in any domain of knowledge that was the principal achievement of this project. This will be illustrated throughout the remainder of this book.

Learning from Our Students How to Help People
Learn to Learn

As my graduate students prepared concept maps to show how children's learning progressed as they studied A-T science lessons, they became very proficient in constructing concept maps. Many of them began to use concept maps to summarize and clarify their own studies in graduate science courses and other courses. I also found that making a concept map of a difficult research paper or section of a textbook was very helpful in clarifying my own ideas and providing me a better understanding of the ideas being presented. It occurred to me in 1978 that our research was suggesting that there were some very helpful things we could teach to Cornell University students that would help them become more powerful learners.

The course I developed drew heavily on what I learned in our research program. I had observed that planning and conducting interviews with students helped my graduate students better understand Ausubel's Assimilation Theory of Learning. They observed that those students who were seeking to understand what they studied had much better organized structure to their knowledge, they could apply their knowledge to new but related problems, and they felt more confident about their knowledge. Building concept maps for the students interviewed helped them to see the hierarchical nature of cognitive structures and gave deeper meaning to Ausubel's idea that most learning involves subsuming and integrating new concepts into more general superordinate concepts. In short, they saw that students who were trying to engage in meaningful learning had more and better organized knowledge and were much more successful in applying their knowledge in new situations.

So, I required all students in my new Learning to Learn course to begin with learning the basic ideas of Ausubel's learning theory and to make a succession of concept maps that illustrated their growing understanding of his theory. I also required them to plan an interview on any subject of interest to them and to interview ten subjects of their own choosing on the subject they had chosen.

Volunteers presented to the class what they were observing as their interviewing and concept mapping progressed, and this helped both the presenter and other students improve their interviews and the quality of their concept maps of interviews. A few students showed video clips from tapes of their interviews, and these were very helpful to everyone. The esprit de corps in the class was excellent, and I looked forward to every class meeting. Each student prepared a final written report on their project that included concept maps for each interview done and whatever other observations they wished to make. An example of one student's project will be presented later in this chapter.

Most of my students who enrolled in my course were juniors or seniors. Initially I was surprised that most of them said they had not written a major paper since Freshman English, and almost all had never presented orally the results of a personal research project. As the semester progressed, all of the students became active participants in the discussions. Given the high standards for Cornell University admission, many of my students indicated that they were not aware there was any other way to learn other than to just memorize as much as possible. This strategy had worked for them in high school and most large Freshman and Sophomore courses. But Cornell University is a great university and most upper division course professors require a higher level of thinking and reasoning. The students who learned primarily by memorizing saw their grades fall from As and Bs to Cs and Ds. That is when they became interested in getting help with their learning strategies.

Lev Vygotsky had pointed out years ago that students can learn better by interacting with their peers. I had all of my students prepare a one-page biography and I shared these with the whole class. This facilitated the process of choosing a "learning partner," since most of the students had previously not known any other class member. Students were asked to share and critique each other's written materials, and a few assignments were explicitly to be done with their learning partner. Many of the complimentary things said about my course by my students included comments on working with a learning partner. In fact, I learned later that at least a few learning partners wound up getting married.

So, if you can do so, may I suggest that you find a learning partner or two to read this book and perform the suggested activities as a team. Even if this team breaks up after a chapter or two, you will have some lasting benefits.

In the twenty years that I taught this course, I never had a student fail to succeed to become a relatively good meaningful learner. I did have about a

10 percent dropout rate, but this was usually because they found the course required more time and/or effort than they were prepared to commit to. Not all courses in the Department of Education required a fairly high degree of commitment and time to perform successfully.

Here are a few things they learned in my Learning to Learn classes that caused this transformation from passive rote learners to active, creative, meaningful learners. First, they were taught key ideas in Ausubel's Assimilation Theory of Learning. They learned that only the learner can choose their learning strategy, and this can vary from simple memorization of information to strong efforts to integrate new concepts and propositions with related ideas they already knew. They also learned that depending on the quality of their existing ideas, the degree of meaningful learning can vary from almost rote learning to very high levels of meaningful learning. Only the learner can choose to learn by rote or by her/his best efforts to accomplish meaningful learning. Therefore, learning is not a simple dichotomy of rote versus meaningful learning; it is a continuum. This continuum was illustrated in Figure 1.4.

The second important idea they were helped to understand is that knowledge in any field is essentially a large body of well-organized concepts and propositions. New knowledge is created either by an individual or by a team. When a new pattern in events or objects is identified or created, this pattern is given a name. In our case, our research team chose to call a hierarchical structure of concepts and propositions a *concept map*. We had invented the concept of a concept map.

Not all of my students found it easy to make their first few concept maps. It soon became evident that those students who had been learning throughout their school years, and even in college, primarily by memorizing information really struggled to make their first acceptable concept map. Some came to my office to discuss dropping the class because they thought they just could not think in the way that was needed to make good concept maps. I assured them that if they learned to talk by age three, they could become very successful at concept mapping knowledge they wanted to understand within a few weeks – and they all succeeded by week 5 or 6 of the course. Some spoke with me about how depressed they were to realize that they had gone through all their past schooling and really understood almost nothing about the subjects they had studied! Remember, these were Cornell University students and most of them were in the top 10 percent of their high school class!

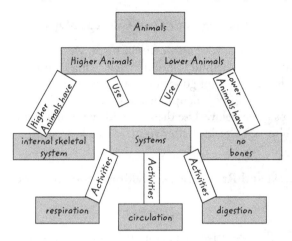

Figure 1.9   A concept map about animal characteristics made using strips of paper, one color for concepts and another for linking words.

In our early work with concept maps from 1972 to 1983, all were drawn using a pen or pencil. We found that even building a good concept map with as few as ten or twelve concepts required two or three revisions. These revisions can be done rather quickly, but when one tries to make a concept map of some more complex topic with twenty to forty concepts, revisions can be frustratingly time consuming. Moreover, our experience was that for almost any more complex topic, at least three or four revisions were needed to obtain a satisfying concept map. Making three or four larger concept maps could become very tedious!

One solution we tried for this problem was to write concepts and linking words on strips of paper and then arranging these on a desk or table. Figure 1.9 shows an example of this. It was a good way to get children started in building concept maps.

In some training sessions we used sticky notes placed on wrapping or butcher paper, so it was easy to move around concepts, but once linking lines with linking words were added, revisions were difficult. It was not until the late 1980s that desktop computers became widely available, and also software specifically designed to do things such as making concept maps.

Our later development of software for laptop computers in the mid-1980s facilitated concept map making, and this was a great boost to our work. The development of excellent concept mapping software by Alberto Cañas and his team will be presented in the next chapter.

Making Your Own Concept Maps

If you have never built your own concept maps, we suggest that you do so now. You may find it helpful to begin by reviewing Figure 1.10 that shows important characteristics of good concept maps. We also recommend that you make a copy of the definitions and ten "rules" for making good concept maps given below. Use these to guide your preparation of concept maps, and also as a checklist after you have made a concept map.

Criteria and Rationale for Making Good Concept Maps

Definitions

CONCEPT: A perceived regularity or pattern in events or objects, or representations of events or objects, designated by a word or symbol.

PROPOSITION: Two or more concepts linked with words to form a statement about how some aspect of the universe appears or acts. Propositions are the units of meaning in meaningful learning and form the structure of a domain of knowledge when well organized and integrated.

Rules for Making Good Maps

1. A context for the concept map should be defined, commonly with a stated explicit "focus question."

Concept maps are very helpful for organizing the knowledge needed to find solutions to problems or questions. These may derive from a topic of study or some form of inquiry. The focus question helps to delineate the knowledge that is most relevant to the problem or question. Stating an explicit question can be very helpful in identifying the best concepts to include at the top level of a concept map. In turn, identifying the best concepts to include at the top of a map often leads to a better, revised focus question. When working in a group setting, the process of identifying a good focus question and the six to ten top-level concepts may take half as much time as constructing the complete initial concept map. A good focus question helps to define clearly the context we are working in and aids in the process of concept mapping the knowledge pertinent to that context. The focus question may appear as the top node of a concept map, or as a header for the map.

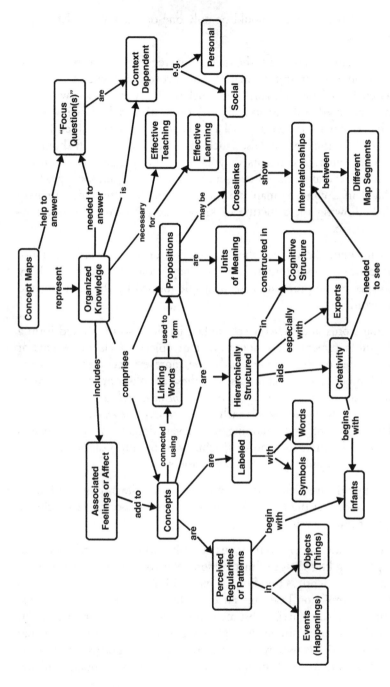

Figure 1.10 A concept map showing the key features of concept maps. More requests were received for publication of this figure than any of the author's other figures.

2. Concept labels in maps should be only one or a few words labeling a specific concept.

Concept labels represent the perceived regularities or patterns in events or objects, or transformations of records of events or objects, designated by a label. Usually, the label is one word or a few words, e.g., history, medieval history, disease, or heart attack. Usually when more than one word is used to label a concept, one must consider if some of the words in the label are also labels for other concepts and should be indicated as separate concepts in your map. Only rarely is a concept indicated by several words. When sentences or longer phrases appear as a node label in a concept map, a submap might be more appropriately included, showing the structure of knowledge represented by the sentence or phrase.

3. Linking lines should be labeled with one or a few words, and not contain concepts labels important to the map's conceptual content. They help to specify the proposition or principle formed by the concepts and linking words.

Linking words and the concepts linked by these words should form a meaningful statement about some event or object, or class of events or objects. More specific linking words give more explicit meaning to the relationship between two concepts, and these are often preferred to more generic linking words such as: *is, a, are, includes, related to,* etc. More specific links may include words such as: *requires, composed of, derived from,* etc. The degree of understanding of a given domain of knowledge is indicated in the precision and/or specificity of the proposition shown in the concepts and linking words given in the map.

4. Maps should have hierarchical organization, with the most general, most inclusive concept at the top, and progressively more specific, less inclusive concepts at lower levels.

There is evidence that our brains store knowledge hierarchically and thus organizing knowledge in this fashion helps to acquire and use knowledge more efficiently. Building a hierarchical structure also follows Ausubel's Assimilation Learning Theory, wherein new knowledge is most easily acquired when it is subsumed under an existing concept in our mind. Evidence from studies of experts versus novices also indicates that acquiring expertise is usually associated with better-organized, more hierarchical map structures. Building such concept maps encourages higher levels of meaningful learning, leading to longer retention of knowledge and greater ability to apply this knowledge in novel settings.

5. In general no more than three or four sub-concepts should be linked below a given concept.

A fundamental consideration operates here: Usually when we find five or more sub-concepts linked under a concept, there are maybe two or more concepts of intermediate generality that can be added to a map, thus increasing the detail and precision of the ideas presented.

6. Specific examples of objects or events may be added to maps where appropriate, but these should clearly be distinguishable from concepts. This may be done by eliminating the concept box or oval being used.

Given the epistemology or theory of knowledge underlying concept maps, it is important to recognize the difference between specific events or objects and concept labels for regularities recognized in specific events or objects. By noting specific examples (not in boxes or other node forms) helps to clarify the kinds of events or objects that are identified by the concept label in the node. On the other hand, numerous examples that are not needed to clarify concept meanings results in a "cluttered" map and thus obscure the structure of knowledge we are trying to elucidate.

7. Crosslinks should specify significant interrelationship between two concepts in different submaps of knowledge shown in the whole map. These are best added when the map is nearing completion.

Creative insights usually result from recognition of new relationships between concepts and/or propositions in one subdomain of a given body of knowledge with those in another subdomain. These kinds of relationships can be indicated by crosslinks in a concept map of sufficient complexity and inclusiveness and can lead to creative insights. Partly for this reason, if we are looking for new creative insights, it is important to plan to build concept maps that are hierarchically well organized and large and complex enough to optimize the chances for identifying significant crosslinks, and yet not so large as to be overwhelming. Otherwise, we might better use submaps.

8. Concept labels should not appear more than once in a given map.

The meaning of a concept is represented by all of the propositions that contain the concept in a given knowledge domain. Thus, to define the meaning explicitly, it is best to use a given concept label only once in a given concept map. A map that contains the same concept two or more times can usually be restructured so that the concept only appears once. Sometimes this may require reconstruction of other sections of the map and usually this leads to general improvement of the map.

9. Resources may be added to concept maps either on concepts or on linking words when using CmapTools software. This software is described in the next chapter.

Resources can be added to concept maps to provide formal definitions of concepts and specific examples, to elaborate further on concept meanings, and attach submaps or other illustrative material. There is always the consideration of whether concept map attachments would be better shown directly as part of the map, or as an attached resource. This is a judgment call and may vary depending on the primary purpose for using the map. Any material that can be digitized may be added as a resource when using CmapTools software.

When resources are attached to linking words, one must always consider whether one or more words in the linking phrase might be better included as additional concepts added to the map structure instead, forming additional concept nodes in a revised map.

10. Additional global maps may be constructed to show crosslinks between concepts on the superordinate and subordinate concept maps. Such global maps may contain fifty or more concepts.

Often in the past, new creative insights have arisen when creative people find new important relationships between concepts in two different subdomains of knowledge. Searching for new crosslinks between concepts in different subdomains on a global concept map for possible crosslinks may increase creative insights.

Begin building your concept map, applying the above rules.

1. Find a page of a book you want to study or an interesting newspaper or journal article or website pages.
2. Select a portion of the document to be mapped.
3. Prepare a "focus question" for the selected content. A focus question indicates what key question is answered by the segment selected, or what key idea is discussed. Your concept map should help to answer the focus question.

4. Identify the key concepts in this piece. While most words are labels for concepts, some are much more pertinent to answering your focus question.

5. Make a "Parking Lot" listing the key concepts selected. If you have already downloaded CmapTools and begun to use this software, the steps that follow will be easier for you.

6. Try to reorder your parking lot items so that the most general, most inclusive concepts are at the top and the least general, most specific concepts are at the bottom.

7. Begin building your concept map, beginning with the top concepts in your Parking Lot.

8. Place all the concepts in your Parking Lot into your map with appropriate linking words. Try to build a good hierarchical structure as you build your map.

9. Add pertinent concepts you may have missed initially.

10. Revise your concept map to make it more precise and more specific. This may require finding more explicit linking words.

11. Check your map against the ten rules for good maps given above.

Revise it again if need be.

An Example: Here is an approach I have used successfully to teach concept mapping to first grade children:

I brought a Geranium plant to the classroom and proceeded to ask the children the names of parts of the plant. I pointed out that each of these words is a concept. Many other flowers may look different, but they may have the same kinds of parts. Here is the list I wrote for the names of these parts on the board as they were suggested:

Concept List (Parking Lot) Elicited from the Students

leaf
flower
stem
plant
petal
nectar
bees
color
green
orange
roots

Next, I indicated that we needed to reorder this list of concepts from those that were biggest or most inclusive down to those that are smaller or most specific. So next we created this "Modified Parking Lot":

plant
stem
leaf
root
green
petal
orange
nectar
bees

I then began to build this concept map on the blackboard starting with plant and asking the children where we could connect, one at a time, the other concepts. They built this concept map:

A week later, I brought in sheets of paper with a list of concepts on the top side and asked the children to use those words to construct a concept map just as the class had done a week earlier. I had five different word lists and children chose one they wanted to use. Every list was chosen by at least one student. The concept map created by Denny is shown in Figure 1.12.

Denny's teacher was impressed with the good thinking evidenced in Denny's map – and with all the maps created by the children.

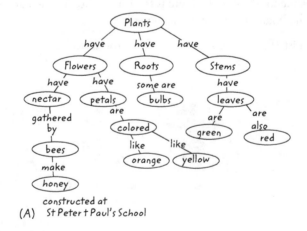

(A)   constructed at
       St Peter t Paul's School

Figure 1.11   A concept map about plants created with a grade 1 class.

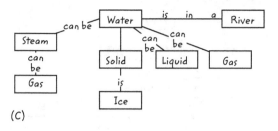

Figure 1.12   A concept map created by Denny, a grade 1 student. This was the first concept map he created.

So now that you have seen what grade 1 children can do in building concept maps, try making a few of you own. Choose any topics of interest to you and try making three or four concept maps. Go back and look at these a few days later and consider what changes you might make to improve each map. Check your map against the ten rules for good maps given earlier. By the end of this work, you should be on the way to becoming a good concept map maker.

Testing Our Tools and Ideas in Other Settings

In August of 1980, I accepted an invitation to be a Fulbright Senior Scholar to lecture in Australia. In recent years I had had several visiting professors from Australia and had enjoyed discussing and debating educational issues with them. All of them were also delightful to socialize with. I was based at Monash University in Melbourne, but I also was committed to lecturing at other universities in Australia as part of my Fulbright Fellowship. In the course of my five months in Australia, I lectured at universities in all Australian states except the Northern Territory. A country almost as big as the USA, Australia had only some 20 million people, so most of the country is sparsely populated "outback" or jungle.

At Monash University, Peter Fensham sponsored a seminar on educational research. I made several presentations at this seminar and received some very critical, but also very encouraging feedback on my *Theory of Education*, published in 1977. There was also extensive discussion on how concept mapping might improve education. One of Fensham's former Ph.D. students, David Symington, worked with elementary school teachers and he wanted to see how concept mapping might facilitate learning in first through third grade classes. Some of the teachers Dave had worked with previously were interested in seeing how concept mapping might help

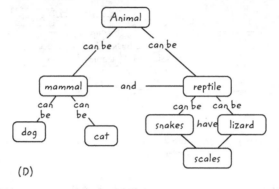

(D)

Figure 1.13   A concept map about animals prepared by a grade 1 student in
Melbourne, Australia, 1980.

their students become better learners. Dave and I introduced students in
grades 1 to 3 to concept mapping and also explained the difference
between rote learning and learning for understanding. Both Dave and
the teachers were impressed with how quickly the children caught on to
concept mapping and how receptive they were to learning ideas about how
to become better learners. These were some of the most encouraging
experiences I had had working with grade 1–3 students, and they added
to my confidence that the learning tools and ideas I and my students had
developed in upstate New York could work anywhere in the world.
A concept map prepared by one of the grade 1 students David and
I worked with is shown in Figure 1.13.

When I returned to the USA, I moved into our condo on Carolina Beach,
North Carolina. I had accepted a position as Distinguished Visiting
Professor at the University of North Carolina in Wilmington. Professor
Joel Mintzes was my sponsor. Although I had agreed to do some lectures
and workshops for the University, my primary activity was to write a draft of
a new book that was published by Cambridge University Press in 1984 with
the title, *Learning How to Learn*. I drew heavily on my experiences teaching
two courses at Cornell University: a graduate course, Theory and Methods
of Education, and an undergraduate course, Learning to Learn, plus my
recent work in Australia and North Carolina. I also wanted to follow up on
my experiences teaching concept mapping to elementary school students in
Australia. Fortunately, I found some of the teachers in Carolina Beach
Elementary School interested in working with me.

The reading specialist at Carolina Beach school was fascinated with
concept maps and she thought they may very well help a student she

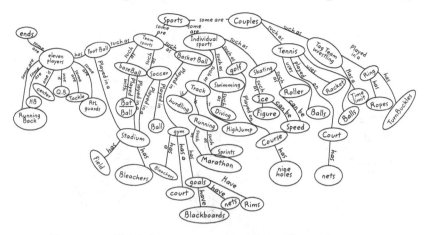

Figure 1.14   Ricky's first concept map prepared to illustrate his concept mapping skill.

had been working with for a couple of years. Ricky was in sixth grade, but he did poorly on reading exams and was in danger of failing promotion into junior high school. I met with Ricky on a Thursday and began by showing him how we can make concept maps for familiar things, similar to the concept map on animals shown in Figure 1.13. Ricky appeared to be interested in working with me, so I asked him if he would make a concept map on something he was interested in. Ricky said he would. I asked what he planned to map, and he said, "motors." When I returned the following Thursday, Ricky showed me the map he made on "Sports." I asked, "What happened to your map on motors?" Ricky said when he started to make this map, he decided he did not know much about motors. But he sure knew a lot about sports!

Ricky showed his map to his teacher, and she was intrigued by it. She said they would be studying feudalism next week and asked if he would read this section of their history book and make a concept map for it. The map Ricky made is shown in Figure 1.15. The teacher was so pleased with it she asked Ricky to present it to the whole class. He did this – and also made concept maps for other things his class was studying. The positive remarks by his teachers and classmates were a great ego boost to Ricky and his performance in all areas of study improved markedly. He was promoted to junior high school in June. This is just one case of hundreds we have experienced where helping learners become better meaningful learners changed the course of their lives.

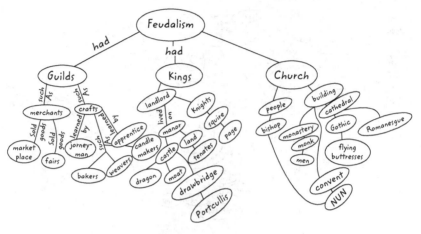

Figure 1.15   Ricky's concept map for a book unit on feudalism. He made a number of other concept maps to guide his class's learning during the remainder of the spring semester.

Learning How to Conduct and Interpret Clinical Interviews

As noted earlier, using clinical interviews with children was the only reliable and valid way we could find to assess children's learning of science concepts. Over the years my research teams became very skilled in conducting and interpreting interviews. Once again, my students were telling me something that I had not incorporated into my earlier work as an educator. Teaching students how to design, conduct, and interpret clinical interviews was a great way to help students become better learners. From the mid-1970s to today, I see learning how to design and use clinical interviews as a major foundation for learning how to be a better learner. Interviewing subjects and concept mapping these interviews provides a window into the cognitive and affective structure of the subjects, insights into the concept/propositional knowledge of the interviewees, and their feelings about this knowledge. Designing, conducting, and evaluating interviews became a major portion in my Learning to Learn course and my Theory and Methods of Education course.

To introduce my students to interviewing, I first showed video clips of interviews done by me and my graduate students working on our twelve-year longitudinal study of children's science learning, and other research projects. Later I also had some good videos of interviews done by students in my classes as part of the required class work.

Prior to planning an interview, I had required my students to learn basic ideas of Ausubel's Assimilation Learning Theory. I also tried to help them understand something about the nature of knowledge, namely that the building blocks of knowledge in any field are concepts and propositions. The essentials of this information were presented earlier in this chapter and were part of the first few weeks of my courses. I also introduced them to one of the few educational principles that research has solidly confirmed, the principle of *wait time.* Mary Budd Rowe (1974) and her students found that, on average, teachers wait only 0.7 seconds for a student to respond to a question before revising the question or asking another student to respond. She called this interval between teacher's questions and student's response or moving to another student or restatement of the question *wait time.* Rowe found that only questions requiring essentially rote recall of information can get valid response with this short wait time. If wait time is increased to at least 3–4 seconds, questions may require more thought and student answers can be more thoughtful. The point I wish to make here is that when doing a good interview, we should ask questions that require some thought and reflection on the part of the interviewee. While some good questions might be responded to in 3–4 seconds, questions that require 15–30 seconds for a thoughtful response result in more thoughtful answers and a better interview.

When you do your first interviews, have a watch or clock in view that clearly shows the seconds elapsed. You may be amazed at how a wait time of 30 seconds really feels like forever. As you gain experience interviewing, you will find you are using better questions, probing more deeply into your interviewee's cognitive and affective memories. You can become comfortable using wait times of 20 to 40 seconds or more.

The challenge for the interviewer is to design questions in such a way that they will elicit the interviewee's concepts and propositional ideas about whatever topic she/he chooses to study. The first step is to prepare a concept map of the domain of knowledge about which you choose to question your subjects. This map will suggest not only the questions you need to ask but also the sequence to use in asking the questions. In general, it is always best to begin with the most general, most inclusive concepts. All interviewees should be able to respond to these questions, whereas many or even most may not be able to respond to questions dealing with relatively minor, specific concepts that might be included in the lower sections of your planning concept map.

It is helpful to select one or more props to use in an interview. The prop may be as simple as a photo or as complex as an apparatus used in studies

Figure 1.16   A grade 12 student being interviewed about materials she studied in a grade 2 A-T lesson.

in this field. Asking pre-planned questions about the props helps to standardize the interview administered to different subjects making comparisons between subjects more valid. Figure 1.16 shows some of the props used in an interview in our twelve-year study. One of my graduate students is interviewing a grade 12 student about materials in a jar dealing with the nature of matter that were studied in grade 2.

Of course, there are always surprises when one begins to interview people about any subject. So, one must be prepared to modify the concept map you began with and then the questions or question sequence. The goal is to get the best possible insight into each subject's concepts and the propositions they think with on this subject. It is also important to try to elicit their feelings about the ideas they present. Later in this book I will discuss other strategies to get insight into the role of feelings in learning and using knowledge.

I required each of my students to select a topic they felt they knew well and to design a clinical interview to be conducted with ten subjects. They were free to select any subject matter and any age group they wanted to work with. Planning, conducting, and analyzing interviews with ten subjects can be very time-consuming, so I urged my students to choose carefully the topic of their study. Planning, conducting, and preparing a report on their study were to be 50 percent of their course grade. My students invested some 30 to 60 hours planning, conducting, and preparing their written report on their project. Student feedback on this work was very positive.

Figure 1.17 is a concept map made by one of my students to guide her in her interviews. I chose this example because it involves both thoughts and feelings. It is also a subject that all of my readers can relate to.

Guided by her concept map, she proceeded to interview ten friends who were willing to cooperate. As she proceeded with her interviews, she found that her subjects placed more emphasis on experiences other than math anxiety, unlike what she had initially expected. In later interviews she probed these alternative thoughts and feelings more than in early interviews. The result is partly evident in the concept map she made for one of her later student interviewees shown in Figure 1.18.

This student found that due to good planning, she was successful in eliciting the thoughts and feelings her ten subjects held about anxiety with the math they had studied. She also found that those subjects who felt the least anxiety about doing math were students who saw ways to use the math they were learning and felt they had mastered the ideas taught. Taken all together, she felt she had gained some good insights about math education. One of her conclusions was that supplementary tools such as workbooks and the use of concept mapping could be helpful in learning math and reducing math anxiety.

Over the years, we have come to appreciate that learning to construct, administer and concept map clinical interviews is not just a tool to be used to help us understand the nature of knowledge and how people store and use knowledge. Acquiring the skill to plan, execute, and evaluate clinical interviews has value in almost every kind of learning challenge you will encounter in your life. As we continue with this chapter and the other chapters of this book, we shall illustrate in case after case how this process was employed to capture and organize knowledge of others in ways that facilitated the use of that knowledge.

Not only were my students learning how to design, conduct, and evaluate interviews, they were also gaining insight on the nature of cognitive learning in human beings. They were observing how the subjects combined concepts to form propositions and how these propositions were organized into hierarchical structures. They were acquiring what has come to be known as *metacognitive knowledge* (Kuhn, 2000), or knowledge about cognitive processes in human beings. They see these knowledge structures

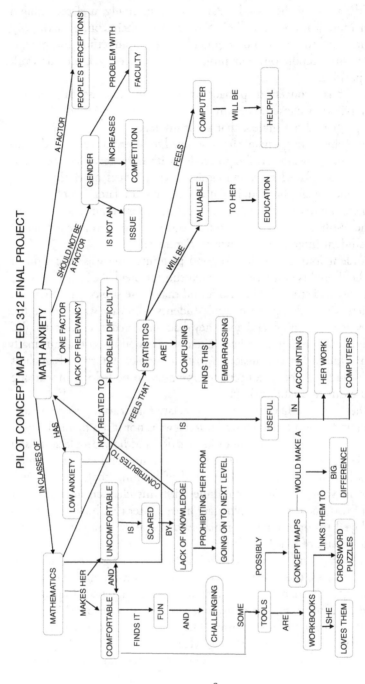

Figure 1.17 A concept map prepared to guide an interview about math anxiety.

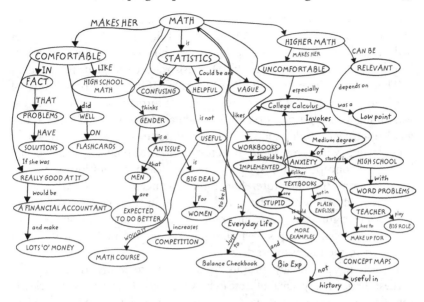

Figure 1.18   A concept map prepared from the transcript of a math interview with one of her students later in her study.

unfolding as they progress through their interviews with subjects. They were also engaged in *meta-knowledge* learning as they see the structure of knowledge unfolding in their interviews. They observed that in the best-informed interviewees, knowledge is organized in hierarchical structures and not in linear strings (Novak, 2010).

Helping People Create New Knowledge

Important as our research team's work over the past sixty years has been for helping people learn in school, work, or informal settings, we believe our greatest achievements have been in developing the theory, ideas, tools, and strategies to help people create new knowledge. As noted earlier in this chapter, we see creative thinking as essentially what occurs with very high levels of meaningful learning. Therefore, the same tools, ideas, and methodologies we have presented to facilitate meaningful learning can be employed to facilitate creative thinking. We present below one example of this done by one of my graduate students at Cornell University.

As a result of successful collaboration on projects that I had done with colleagues in plant biology at Cornell University, I was able to persuade one professor to encourage his students to use concept mapping to assist in planning, conducting, and reporting their Ph.D. research. Christi Palmer had studied with me, and she decided to see how concept mapping might help her plan and conduct her Ph.D. thesis research in plant pathology.

There was an interest in the Plant Pathology Group at Cornell to see if they could find some way to retard or prevent formation of grey mold that was killing a number of crop and ornamental plants. Christi began as any good researcher would; she studied all the pertinent literature she could find dealing with grey mold infections and treatments. Christi began building a concept map to show all the key ideas and questions she could identify from the literature. She built a concept map showing what concepts and propositions she found validated in the literature, and where there were significant questions remaining. She identified six possible linkages between concepts regarding preventing grey mold that were not answered in the literature to date.

Identifying potentially promising questions to study is usually the hardest part in any area of research. Once good questions are clearly specified, it is usually relatively easy to conduct the research needed to answer these questions. Unlike the field of education and some other fields, most fields of science have well developed theories, principles, and methodologies for solving problems and answering questions.

Christi did the necessary experiments and reported what she found in her Ph.D. thesis. In her final oral exam, her graduate committee complimented her on the quality of her thinking and clarity of her report on the results of her studies. The concept map Christi developed to guide her research is shown in Figure 1.19.

In subsequent chapters, we will build further on the foundations developed above to help you build your understanding of how we learn and how we create new knowledge. In the following chapters, we will take you through our continuing journey to help people learn up to the most recent work we and others are doing. This will include new educational strategies that show promise.

The evolution of personal computers and the development of the World Wide Web had not yet occurred when I wrote *Learning How to Learn* in 1981. The Digital Revolution was yet to come. The impact of this revolution on teaching and learning transformed our world, and this process continues today. The explosive development of cell phone technology is in many ways even more revolutionary, allowing anyone to hold virtually all of the knowledge in the world in the palm of their hand. What we hope to do with this book is help you see new ways to benefit from

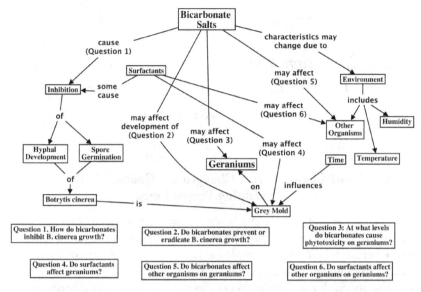

Figure 1.19   Christi Palmer's concept map on bicarbonate salts is based on pertinent literature and her six Ph.D. thesis research questions derived from concept mapping key ideas in the literature (Palmer, 1996).

these extraordinary developments. We cannot even imagine what the next Apple or Facebook company will do to open up better ways to help people learn. We can be certain that more revolutionary changes will come in technology, and these will have profound effects on how people learn and how they interact with one another.

In the next chapter, I shall describe some of the things that we have done at IHMC that are having a very positive impact on efforts to help people learn.

CHAPTER 2

The Invention and Use of CmapTools Software in Schools, Corporations, and Other Organizations

A Series of Chance Events Changed the Course of My Efforts for Helping People Learn

In the summer and fall of 1986, I was considering possible places I might go on sabbatical leave during the following school year. I do not recall just where or when I again met Bruce Dunn, a former Cornell University Ph.D. student in Educational Psychology. Bruce suggested I consider coming to the University of West Florida where he was a professor of psychology. The University of West Florida (UWF) is in Pensacola, Florida, about ten miles north from Pensacola Beach on the Gulf of Mexico. My wife and I had been considering future retirement places and we thought the idea of living on Pensacola Beach for seven to eight months might be a good opportunity to consider this as a future winter home. I also thought that Bruce and I could do some good research together.

Bruce was doing research using equipment he had assembled to record electroencephalographic brain images under various conditions of mental activity. This equipment allowed an investigator to record electrical signals produced by different regions of the brain during mental activities of various kinds (see Figure 2.1). Such studies are called electroencephalography (EEG). It uses electrodes placed on the scalp to record electrical signals produced by brain activity recorded during mental tasks. EEG can be used in cognitive research or to diagnose medical conditions such as epilepsy and sleep disorders. We thought it might be interesting to see how EEG activity might vary when children were engaged in different mental tasks using concept maps. Some of the results of our studies were published in 1989 (Dunn et al., 1989). The only point I want to make now is that we found clear evidence that EEG readings were definitely related to the complexity of the children's concept mapping activity. I will discuss this further in another chapter.

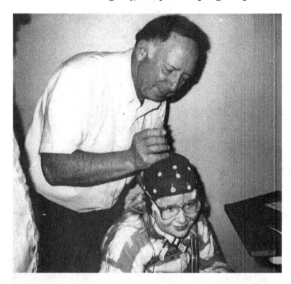

Figure 2.1   The author is preparing a grade 5 child to record EEG brain activity while she performs some tasks with a concept map she created.

A longtime friend of Bruce Dunn, Dr. Kenneth Ford (see Figure 2.2), joined the faculty of Computer Science in the fall of 1987. Bruce urged Ken to look into what I was doing with concept maps. At first, Ken was skeptical, since he had a very low opinion of anyone working in the field of educational research. After a few sessions with Ken, he became intrigued with the possibilities that concept mapping might help with one of the most basic problems in Artificial Intelligence (AI), Ken's field of research. Ken believed that the problem in AI is to identify explicitly the knowledge held by an expert in any given domain of knowledge. Ken thought the use of concept maps could be one good solution to this problem.

Ken had been working with a local cardiologist, Dr. Andrews, who had developed a technology for assessing human coronary problems that he called First Pass Functional Imaging (FPFI). The major problem he had in spreading the use of the technology was in training cardiologists to use this technology successfully. He had authored a book on how to employ FPFI, but this did not solve the problem of training more cardiologists to use his system. He had approached Ken to see if an AI approach might be more successful for training cardiologists.

We began by making a concept map based on the material in Andrews' book on the use of his technology. In this work, we found that there were some sections of our concept map that we were not sure what linking

Figure 2.2   Ken Ford has served as the director of IHMC since its founding in 1989.

words would be best for these segments of our concept map. We subsequently conducted interviews with Andrews and clarified some ideas that were not clear or were simply missing in our original map. It turned out that a few key concepts were not well presented in his book and were missing in our initial concept map. I recall that after one of my interviews with Andrews, he asked if I was a cardiologist. What allowed me to ask explicit questions to clarify some of the uncertainties we had with our initial concept maps was, however, not any training in medicine but my years of experience interviewing experts and preparing concept maps of their knowledge.

Once we had developed a concept map that dealt with all the key ideas one needed in order to understand the process of FPFI, it was relatively easy to prepare an AI training program that could be used to train other cardiologists. We had access to videotapes that Andrews had on file from previous case studies, and for which he had also conducted analysis of the coronary problems identified. We used these tapes to test and refine the AI training program as development proceeded. We found that at the end of the AI program development, the accuracy by our project staff in diagnosing additional cases of heart disease was very high. The remarkable result was that the training program we developed was so effective that in 93 percent of the cases reviewed by our AI staff, they made the correct diagnosis. Cardiologists trained by the original textbook-based training programs had only about a 50 percent success rate in their diagnoses – far too low for actual use with patients (Ford et al., 1991).

Ford became convinced that concept mapping had much to offer to the world of AI and especially to the community interested in problems of expert knowledge acquisition. We published in 1991 two papers describing ICONKAT: An Integrated Constructivist Knowledge Acquisition Tool that presented the underlying theory as well as the ways to use concept maps for knowledge acquisition. This and other papers were well received by researchers in the field of AI (Ford et al., 1991).

The success of our work with Dr. Andrews also led to numerous new projects to capture and use expert knowledge using concept maps. Some of these projects will be discussed later in this chapter and in other chapters, but first we must pause to relate another fortunate chance occurrence in my work.

The Invention of CmapTools Software

Dr. Alberto Cañas (see Figure 2.3), a good friend of Ken Ford, joined the staff in late 1990 at the University of West Florida and the recently formed Institute for Human and Machine Cognition. His work in creating CmapTools software, based partly on my work, was eventually the most significant advance in my efforts to help people learn.

Alberto had been working on a project funded by International Business Machines (IBM) to create software that would allow students in eleven Latin countries to build concept maps and also to incorporate ideas from other students. The participating schools were located in cities near IBM offices where they could call in to access the IBM network, VNet, to share information in both text and pictorial forms. The World Wide Web had not yet been developed. IBM also provided some computers to schools for student use. The project created a software program they called Cmap that permitted students to construct concept maps and to share all or parts of their concept maps with students in other schools. However, this software

Figure 2.3   Alberto Cañas led the team that created CmapTools software.

could be used only on certain IBM computers, and this had limited potential especially at that time.

When I began to spend more time at IHMC in the 1990s, Ken and Alberto began to get funding from the Department of Navy, NASA, and other organizations to advance their work. We began work on a new software program for building concept maps that could be used on almost any computer. Advances in programming languages and desktop computers were making it possible to create concept mapping software that could be used on almost any computer. There were also huge advances in the World Wide Web, providing easy access on almost any topic anywhere in the world.

The guidelines for developing concept maps presented in Chapter 1 were originally developed to help guide programmers working with Alberto to develop CmapTools software. Later in this chapter I will discuss some of the projects in which we used concept mapping as the principal tool. The needs of the various IHMC sponsors required continuous modification and improvement of the software. Alberto led the team that did the many revisions and improvements to CmapTools software.

The most important improvement in CmapTools was the addition of a patented feature not found in any similar software – Alberto and his team had figured out a way to add access to any digital resource by simply dragging the icon for that resource and dropping it onto a concept or linking word in a concept map. This resource then becomes part of the file for the

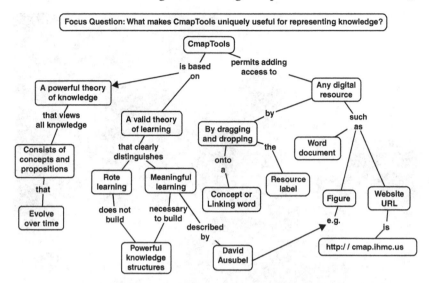

Figure 2.4   A concept map about a few key features of CmapTools.

concept map and can be easily accessed at a later time by simply clicking on the icon for the resource. This is illustrated in Figure 2.4 with the icon on the Ausubel concept that produces his photo when clicked.

As is true with the development of any complex software program, CmapTools was created and refined over a span of years, and indeed it continues to be modified and improved today. Alberto and his team combined their work on CmapTools with work on numerous projects that employed this technology, and these projects provided most of the funding needed for this development. Figure 2.5 shows most of the thirty-eight team members that worked on CmapTools over the years. The original building housing IHMC is in the background. With Ken Ford and Advisory Board leadership, IHMC obtained funding for a much larger additional facility dedicated in 2016.

Getting Started Using CmapTools

If you have not already done so, go to the CmapTools website (http://cmap.ihmc.us) (see Figure 2.6), register and download CmapTools to your computer. There is no charge for this software. You will be simultaneously registered to receive news items and updates for CmapTools. There is also an iPad version, but this has a small charge. I think the laptop version is

Figure 2.5   The CmapTools development team. Alberto Cañas is in the white shirt
in the far right, and the author is in a white shirt in the middle.

Figure 2.6   CmapTools website. Sign in and download CmapTools software at no cost.
Other resources can also be downloaded at this site, including guidance for
building concept maps.

easier to use, and I will make reference only to the laptop version. I use a Mac Pro laptop.

There are other things available at this website, including access to thousands of research papers dealing with the use of concept maps in a wide variety of settings. I suggest you explore some of these items when you have an hour or two to do so.

Ken Ford and Alberto Cañas decided that since CmapTools software was developed primarily with Federal funding, IHMC would make this software available to anyone at no cost. The software can be downloaded by anyone at: http://cmap.ihmc.us. This decision makes for universal availability of the software, but it does not provide funding to maintain the website and upgrades to the software as technologies advance. IHMC accepts small donations for this work from users of the software.

At the time of writing, some 40,000 copies of CmapTools have been downloaded from this site every month. Many thousands more copies are downloaded from other servers located all over the world (see Figure 2.7). IHMC also provides the software for creating a server at no cost.

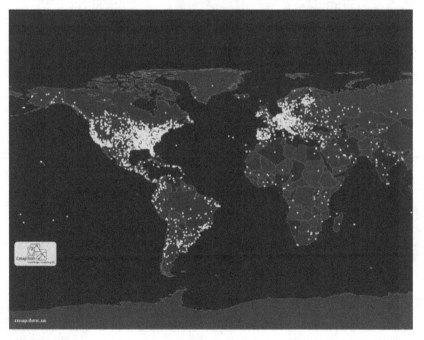

Figure 2.7   Locations around the world where CmapTools were downloaded in one month.

CmapTools' popularity in schools and universities around the world is due in part to research that has shown that the use of concept mapping facilitates meaningful learning. Al-Kunifed and Wandersee (1990) did a review of 100 research studies that employed concept mapping, and almost uniformly these studies found significant facilitation of meaningful learning. CmapTools has made the use of concept mapping in school settings far easier and even more effective (Cañas et al., 2001; Cañas and Novak, 2004, 2008).

As is true for any new software, the only way to gain proficiency with the software is to start playing around with it and gradually learn how to use more of the features of the software. IHMC has prepared various aids for beginners that can be downloaded by clicking on items at the top of the home page. Some short videos on the use of the software are available by clicking on "Docs and Support" at the top of the home page. Also refer to the suggestions made in Chapter 1 for creating good concept maps. We have found that anyone familiar with using software such as MS Word can learn to use CmapTools in a few hours. However, concept maps have so many potential uses that you will never finish learning new ways to use these tools. In fact, you may create some of your own new ways to use CmapTools. And we hope you will share what you have discovered with others in the CmapTools community. Ideally, we hope you will participate in a future international conference on concept mapping. These are held biennially in various countries. For information on the conferences, just Google: International Conference on Concept Mapping. There have also been many published reviews of research on the use of concept mapping such as an early one done by Al-Kuzz and Wandersee (1990).

An early enthusiast for concept mapping was Geoffrey Briggs, Director of NASA's Center for Mars Exploration at the NASA Ames Research Center California. It may interest you to know that some of Geoff's first concept maps showed the same kinds of "errors" as I saw in my Cornell University student's first maps, such as important concepts placed as linking words, more than one concept in a concept node, and poor hierarchy in the concept map structure. However, after my feedback on just a few of these concept maps, Geoff began to send me excellent concept maps, such as the one shown below in Figure 2.8. He became very adept at creating concept maps and attaching a wide range of digital resources to his maps. He prepared over 200 concept maps dealing with Mars Exploration, a program he directed at NASA. Later he went on to prepare a whole series of concept maps dealing with all fields of science.

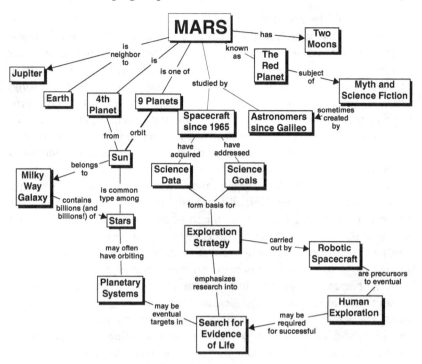

Figure 2.8 This "Top Map" for Mars Exploration serves to access over 100 concept maps on Mars Exploration created by Geoffrey Briggs.

In the past two decades, the IHMC connection has enlarged its research focus to the area of robotics and related disciplines. Robotics is the science that combines ideas and methods from the world of engineering and the world of computer science to create robots that can do many of the things human beings do, including things they cannot do such as working in very low or very high temperatures or in environments with little or no oxygen. There is no doubt that robotics will become very important in the lives of everyone in the future. However, this subject is beyond the scope of this book. You may want to follow some of the exciting work IHMC is doing with robotics by visiting their website: www.ihmc.us.

Helping People in the Business World Learn

Alan McAdams, a professor in the Johnson School of Business at Cornell University, had learned of my work and thought some of the things I was teaching would benefit students in his school. In 1991, he invited me to co-teach a course with him for MBA and Ph.D. students in the Business School. We offered the new course to eighteen students in the fall semester of 1991. McAdams introduced the students to changes that were occurring in the business world, including an accelerating interest in creating, utilizing, and archiving knowledge. I introduced them to Ausubel's learning theory and how to do concept mapping and structured interviews. We organized teams of two to four students to interview leaders and staff in several businesses, and each team made class presentations as their work progressed.

One of the first business organizations we studied was the computer sales organization on the Cornell University campus. Kym Fraser led the group that interviewed all staff members of the computer sales office and prepared concept maps from the interviews. Fraser chose to continue the study with this business group, and it became the basis for her doctoral thesis (1993) and later for a paper (Fraser and Novak, 1998).

What became conspicuous in every case was that there were serious gaps in communicating goals, strategies, and organization problems. In some cases, the variety of understandings of organization goals bordered on shocking, and working with our student groups helped to resolve many of the problems identified. To our surprise, our "experimental course" received the highest ranking by students of any course offered in the Business School in 1991–1992. I continued to participate in this course until I retired in 1995. McAdams continued to offer the course until he retired in 2010.

My experiences with the course we did in the Business School convinced me that the ideas and tools we had developed to better educate people in schools and universities were also valuable when applied in the business world. I began to explore opportunities to work with corporations that might be interested in working with me. A door was opened for me in 1993 when I met Larry Huston, Vice President for Knowledge and Innovation at Procter & Gamble (P&G) in Cincinnati, Ohio.

Huston indicated in a lecture he gave to a meeting of professors that he was looking for new tools that could enhance creativity at P&G. I gave him two of my papers I had brought with me. To my surprise, I had a message on my phone from Huston when I returned to my room after lunch. He asked if I could meet in his office later in the afternoon, and I immediately agreed to do so. Huston asked if my tools and ideas could help research teams at P&G better solve problems with improving or creating new products. I assured him that this was possible.

It was several months before I heard back from Huston. I learned years later that Huston was skeptical that a professor of education could have anything of value to offer. Huston's assistant, Ed Rogers, had family ties to Cornell University and he was familiar with some of my work. He had urged Houston to give my ideas a try at P&G. Once again chance played a role in advancing my work. Huston asked if we could create a concept map with his team that might lead to a solution to their problem in a one-day session. I assured him I thought this was possible. Huston proceeded with the necessary confidentiality paperwork, and a meeting was planned.

I met with a team of eighteen researchers who had been working to develop a new paper product for some two years, without success. We met at 8:00 a.m. on December 28. I thought the initial reception was rather cool (who wants to go to a dubious meeting during Christmas week?). I also learned several weeks later that I was lecturer number 7 or 8 who had brought "a new way for creative thinking" to this group, none of which was successful.

In the first hour of our meeting, I explained the ideas from Ausubel's learning theory and my constructivist views on the nature of knowledge and knowledge creation that are the foundations for concept mapping. The group appeared mildly interested and some good questions were asked. We then proceeded as a group to identify a good focus question for the group's problem and a dozen or so concepts that were critically important for producing this new product. As a group, we built a concept map on an overhead projector, making changes as we went along. By lunchtime, we had built a concept map with some twenty-five concepts.

After lunch, we divided the group into three subgroups and asked them to work as a team on one section of the large map where they felt they were most qualified. Ed Rogers and I assisted the small groups in building their concept maps. Within an hour and a half, each group had built an elaborate concept map for their section of the larger group map. They also had added some additional notes and a submap or two. The work of each subgroup was then presented to the whole group. I pulled the submaps together on an overhead transparency to recreate a larger group map. (Good software for making concept maps was not yet available to this group.) There was a consensus that the concept map represented the key ideas needed to create the new product, but some additional expertise was also needed that was not represented in the group.

It was now evident that the new product would involve the use of hydrophilic gels, and although P&G had several scientists with expertise in this area, none had been assigned to this group. They also agreed that the approaches they were previously pursuing could not be successful. The team leader was satisfied that he could now see a path to a solution for their project, and indeed, within two months they succeeded in creating the new product and they were ready to do test marketing. (Confidentiality agreements do not permit me to show this concept map, or any others created at P&G.)

A second project I did with P&G dealt with some problems they were having with bleaches. Once again, we found that a one-day session with the Bleach Team was sufficient to create a concept map that would show the direction for product improvements. Several weeks after this session I was interviewing some of the participants in our P&G product improvement sessions to get their thoughts on the positive or negative aspects of the sessions. One woman I interviewed had been part of the Bleach Team for only two months. She commented that she had worked in hair care for two years and never felt that she really understood her role with the Hair Care group. She thought she had a better understanding of her role with the work of the Bleach Team after our one-day session building a concept map for their problems. I recall that, during our session, she said that as a dye chemist, she could look at a stain on clothes not just as a stain but rather as a dye, and there were a number of important principles of dye chemistry that could be brought to bear on the bleach problems. Her insights brought new problem solutions to the work of the Bleach group. Thus began a several year venture with P&G, and this led to a whole series of projects with other corporations and organizations.

In 1995, Ikujiro Nonaka and Hirotaka Takeuchi published their book, *The Knowledge Creating Company*. The CEO of Procter & Gamble, John Pepper, was very impressed with the book and urged all his senior officers to read it. Huston pointed out to Pepper that the work we were doing together was indeed making P&G a better knowledge creating company. Pepper asked Huston and I to meet with the board of directors to present our current work.

We presented a large concept map that had just been completed by my team dealing with vaginal infections. P&G was exploring possible new products to deal with this common problem in post-menopausal women. Pepper looked at the map and said: "I don't know anything about post-menopausal infections, but it is obvious to me that vaginal pH and Lactobacillus must be important since so many lines connect to these two things." And indeed, these are important, since pH (acidity) rises after menopause and this favors proliferation of monilial, the yeast that causes the vaginal problems. Lactobacillus is a natural defense against monilial, but it does not do well at higher pH. In the end, P&G did not pursue creating a new product to fight monilial, perhaps because drinking cranberry juice and taking the over the counter, inexpensive probiotic Acidophilus can usually control vaginal infection.

Pepper commented that he had spent the morning on the phone with the Federal Department of Agriculture (FDA) regarding questions they had about several P&G applications submitted for FDA approval. He asked me if I thought we could make a concept map that would help P&G people to write better FDA applications. I assured him that with the right people helping, this could be done. A week or two later I received a call from Ray Ludwa, a person who had been in one of my previous P&G sessions. He asked if I remembered Chairman Pepper's question about creating a concept map that might help P&G people write better FDA applications for approval of new products. Ray Ludwa said Pepper had asked him to create the concept map on FDA applications as we had discussed earlier, and he needed my help. We worked with a team Ludwa identified and created the concept map that he later used successfully to train P&G employees in writing better FDA proposals.

My work with P&G began to decline after 1998 when we had trained a group of P&G staff to do most of what my team had been doing. Partly the decline was due to Dirk Jager becoming the CEO in 1999. Jager was not a supporter of our work. Fortunately, he lasted less than a year and John Pepper was reappointed CEO. By this time, I had moved on to do more work with the Florida Institute for Human and Machine Cognition.

Huston had mentioned in his talk where I first met him that he approached the director of the National Institutes of Health (NIH) in Washington, DC to learn if they had any tools that could improve research productivity in general. The director remarked that he knew of no such tools and if Huston found some, he would be interested in learning what they are. I have no reason to believe that Huston followed up on this request. I considered a possible follow-up with the NIH director, but I had begun to be too busy with other work I shall discuss below.

Perfecting Strategies for Knowledge Elicitation and Application to Problem-Solving

During the five plus years that I worked with Procter & Gamble, I became increasingly aware of the importance of all three aspects of human experience, thinking, feeling, and acting. While all the previous work we had done considered all three of these, the consequences of failure to address adequately any one of these domains could be very costly to the company.

Prior to my work, P&G had developed Olestra, a fat substitute that had all the properties of cooking oil, but since it was not digested by humans, it did not have the caloric or coronary disease negatives associated with commonly used cooking oils. P&G saw a huge market for this product for use in everything from potato chips to bakery and vegetable products. In 1996, I tried some potato chips made with Olestra that were offered in the cafeteria at the P&G Ivorydale facility in Cincinnati, Ohio. On each occasion, I experienced indigestion and a "heavy feeling" in my stomach and intestines. As it turned out, I was not alone in experiencing these uncomfortable side effects from ingesting Olestra. The company later stopped selling the product. There are no good figures on the losses suffered with manufacturing this product, but the plant that made Olestra was sold in 2000. One cannot put a dollar value on the public relations cost of this product, but it would have been substantial.

I noted earlier that when I first introduced concept mapping as a tool to facilitate problem-solving at P&G, I gave a brief introduction to the theoretical foundations of our work that led to our current theory on human learning and problem-solving. In that presentation I mentioned that high levels of meaningful learning that lead to creative work involve successful integration of thinking, feeling, and acting. I thought at the time that the group was receptive to what I offered in terms of the importance of meaningful learning, as contrasted to rote learning, for high levels of creative problem-solving. There appeared to be little reaction to my ideas on the actions needed, and they appeared to ignore my comments on the role of feelings. Over the years that I worked with P&G teams, Larry Huston and some of his associates became much more interested in the importance of achieving optimal levels of all three, thinking, feeling, and acting. In fact, Huston formed his own model for successful creative work as necessitating the coordination of Mind, Body, and Heart. We began developing video-tapes to introduce our evolving strategies to new research and marketing teams, and these included an emphasis on mind, body, and heart. It was about this time that CEO John Pepper retired. He was succeeded by Dirk Jaeger, and this soon ended the team effort with Huston.

In the years I worked with P&G I was very gratified by how well the ideas, theory, and tools we develop in our work in education could be applied in the business world. Moreover, my work with the Institute for Human and Machine Cognition was proving that the tools and ideas we had developed worked equally well with problems faced by business and governmental organizations, and these tools and ideas were being adopted all over the world.

I will always feel indebted to Procter & Gamble and to Larry Huston for the opportunities they extended to me to teach and learn with them. On one visit to Cincinnati in 2003, when we were exploring a new collaboration with Huston, we had a delightful dinner at Huston's home. It was the first time Joan and I had been met at the door by a butler, and had dinner served by a maid. Huston remarked to Joan and I when he drove us back to our motel: "Joe, P&G has made a ton of money applying your tools and ideas." Coming from a man who rarely complimented anyone, both Joan and I were pleased.

Huston retired from Procter & Gamble a few years later and formed his own business consulting company, 4iINNO. He is managing director of the company and also holds an appointment with the Wharton School of Business. His lecture fees run from $30,000 to $50,000. He sent me some examples of concept maps he had created with clients early in his new business career, and they were remarkably complex. He currently lectures and does consulting work all over the world.

The Use of CmapTools Becomes More Widespread Internationally

While I began reducing my business consulting after 2007, others whom I did not know at that time were greatly increasing their use of concept maps in the business world. Thomas Frisendal is a consultant to businesses and other organizations. He is based in Copenhagen, Denmark. He became familiar with some of my earlier writings and began developing strategies to use concept mapping as one tool in his consulting work. In 2012 Frisendal published a book, *Design Thinking Business Analysis: Business Concept Mapping Applied (Management for Professionals)*, presenting the strategies he had developed and encouraging other business consults to consider employing similar strategies. His book contains numerous examples of concept maps he has used in his work with businesses and other organizations.

The Denmark government had passed a new law organizing the labor offices across the country in new ways. Many stakeholders affected by the law were confused about how the new law applied to them. Frisendal conducted a workshop for the state employment authority and together they drafted the concept map shown in Figure 2.9. This proved to be a useful guide for the development of future employment in the sector.

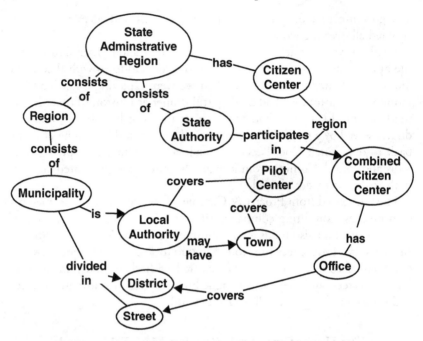

Figure 2.9   The State Administrative Region concept map was done in the initial stages of understanding and clarifying a new law in Denmark organizing the labor offices across the country in new ways.

As Frisendal's consulting work continued, he developed new strategies in addition to the use of concept mapping. He presented these strategies in a second book, *Graph Data Modeling for NoSQL and SQL: Visualize Structure and Meaning* (2016). Both of his books are available at Amazon and other vendors.

Some of the associates who worked with Frisendal have moved on to develop their own consulting businesses and they, too, are finding concept maps to be a useful powerful tool. In fact, Frisendal indicated to me in one of our conversations that most of the business consultants he knows, who work in Scandinavian countries, make some use of the concept mapping tools.

In the USA, a number of business consulting organizations are using CmapTools as part of their work. Brian Moon, Robert Hoffman, Alberto Cañas, and I coauthored *Applied Concept Mapping: Capturing, Analyzing and Organizing Knowledge*. We were joined by twenty-two additional authors who contributed to chapters in this book. The readership for this book includes academics interested in new ways to capture and use knowledge as well as business leaders who see value in building these skills. Brian Moon is also president of Perigean Technologies, a firm dedicated to building innovative software to further enhance the uses of CmapTools.

Moon is leading efforts to develop better evaluation tools. They are searching for better ways to use concept maps and to develop machine scoring methods to facilitate large-scale use of concept maps and other evaluation tools in large-scale testing, such as national school achievement tests. They are strong advocates for the use of concept mapping in schools as an evaluation tool, as opposed to multiple choice-based testing. Their recent work can be accessed through the Internet using search terms such as "Beyond Multiple Choice" and "Use of concept maps for evaluation" (www.serolearn.com).

Fortunately for me, the earlier work that I had begun with IHMC was beginning to expand substantially and I turned my efforts primarily to work with IHMC.

Helping NASA with a Research Program in Astrobiology

In late 1998, IHMC was asked to help with the NASA research program in astrobiology. Since this was a subject of interest to me, and also in my area of expertise, I was asked to help with the project. The research program was based at Moffett Field, California, near San Francisco. The project directors believed that the research teams in the program could better coordinate their research and they thought that concept maps could be a useful tool to help do this. Astrobiology deals with questions about life in outer space.

Cornell University was one of the leaders in the field of astrobiology, and I had some professional and personal ties to this work. Some of my graduate students had worked with Professors Frank Drake and Carl Sagan, two of the international leaders in the area of space exploration. Under their leadership, Cornell University helped to design, build, and manage the 305-meter radio telescope nestled in mountains near Arecibo, Puerto Rico (see Figure 2.10). My daughter began studies at Cornell University with Carl Sagan as her advisor, until he began essentially full-time work on the Nova PBS television series on space exploration. On one trip to Puerto Rico, Joan and I had the opportunity to ride the cable car that takes personnel from the ground to the radio wave receptors suspended above the center of the large disc. This remained the largest radio telescope in the world until China completed a 500-meter radio telescope in 2016.

Radio waves can travel vast distances through space, and certain frequencies of radio waves are considered to be the most likely carriers of messages from outer space if intelligent life exists somewhere else in the universe. The NASA-supported Astrobiology program has as one of its missions the Search for Extra-Terrestrial Intelligence, or the SETI mission. Incidentally, as of this writing, no such signals have been found, but space is vast, and we may be looking for the wrong kinds of signals. There are reasons to believe that life of some kind exists on other planets or planet moons. However, if that intelligent life is a few hundred million years more advanced than we, they may have vastly better communication tools than we know about today. Radio waves may be an obsolete technology for them.

The Aricebo radio telescope suffered serious damage during the summer 2017 hurricane season; however, the telescope was further damaged due to the age of the cables and was decommissioned in 2021. The Chinese radio telescope, almost four times larger, began operations in 2016. Time will tell if China made a good investment in this telescope.

Returning to the work at Moffett Field, there were about twenty separate research projects, each with a team leader, several researchers, and support staff. I began my work by first interviewing the program leader

Figure 2.10   The radio telescope in Arecibo, Puerto Rico showing the 305 meter "lens" of the telescope and the signal receivers suspended over the center of the radio wave reflector disc. (Stocktrek/Photodisc/Getty Images).

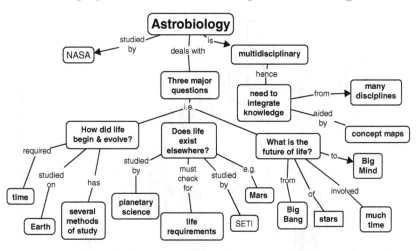

Figure 2.11   Astrobiology Top Map showing three major research questions and their relationships to the key areas of research in astrobiology.

to obtain a general picture of the program's goals. I then interviewed each of the research team leaders to get more detailed aspects of each specific research area. The concept map in Figure 2.11 shows basic questions and related areas in the field of astrobiology as presented to me by the program leader.

Currently scientists believe that the universe began about 13.8 billion years ago. It began from a single very dense, very hot primordial ball that exploded sending matter and energy throughout what we now observe as the universe of stars and galaxies. This explosion is also known as the Big Bang. Our sun and the planets surrounding it were probably formed about 3.5 billion years ago. How life originated and whether or not it can exist elsewhere in the universe are two basic questions studied by astrobiologists. They also study a third question dealing with the possibility of intelligent life elsewhere in the universe. Needless to say, these are not easy questions to answer and they will probably never be answered completely.

After my interview with the director of the Astrobiology Program, I began a series of interviews with the leaders of various project research specialty areas. The leader of the group doing research on archaebacteria was the first research group leader I interviewed, and her concept map is shown in Figure 2.12.

Another effort requested by the Astrobiology Program leader was to see if I could prepare a comprehensive concept map that would combine key

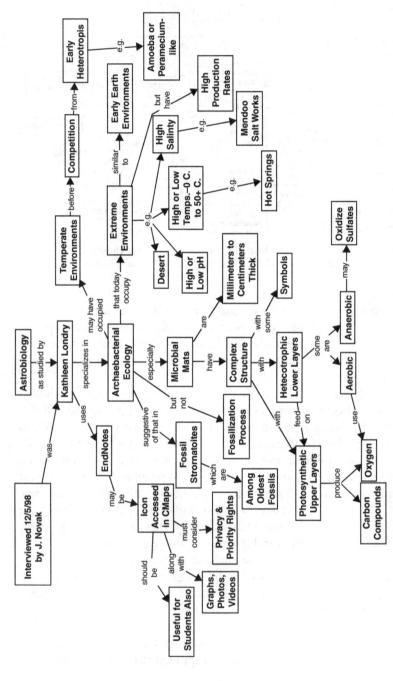

Figure 2.12 A concept map made from an interview with the leader of the Archaebacterial Ecology research project. Some details specific to this program were not included here.

ideas and activities of all the individual project areas into one concept map. The goal here was to prepare a "global" concept map that would suggest some of the possible areas of collaboration that might be identified. My experience had been that any concept map with over 100 concepts plus linking words becomes too overwhelming to be useful for most people. Bearing this in mind, I prepared the concept map in Figure 2.13. Printed on a 12x18 inch paper, the concept map proved to be useful to individual project research teams as well as to the Astrobiology team as a whole. This and other concept maps also served to help communicate the work of the Astrobiology Program to other program areas in NASA and also to the general public.

Although the text may be too small to read on the map in Figure 2.13 in the format used here, the figure does illustrate the complexity of the Astrobiology Program. If I tried to explain what the Astrobiology Program is all about in text, it would probably take forty to fifty pages to describe all the relationships that are shown in this concept map. Moreover, our minds are just not very good at processing linear text, so I doubt that most readers could get a comprehensive understanding of the various research projects and their relationships from such a text.

Understanding Weather Forecasting: Our Early Work

The US Weather Bureau in Pensacola, Florida, had approached the IHMC for help in training weather forecasters. Robert Hoffman, an experimental psychologist, had joined IHMC in 1999 and he was interested in working on the weather forecasting problem. Hoffman had been working on knowledge elicitation projects prior to coming to IHMC, but he had never used concept mapping. We began with me interviewing one of two senior weather forecasters who worked in the Pensacola branch. As my interview proceeded, Robert used the then current version of CmapTools to create a concept map of the forecaster's ideas about "Forecasting Storms," a topic of great interest in Florida (see Figure 2.14).

What we found was that the methods I had developed in my work with Procter & Gamble were easily transferred to work with other organizations. Thus, we began a very successful series of projects helping teams in many organizations to capture and better use expert knowledge more effectively.[1]

---

[1] Additional examples of the concept maps produced on weather forecasting can be seen in Hoffman et al. (2006).

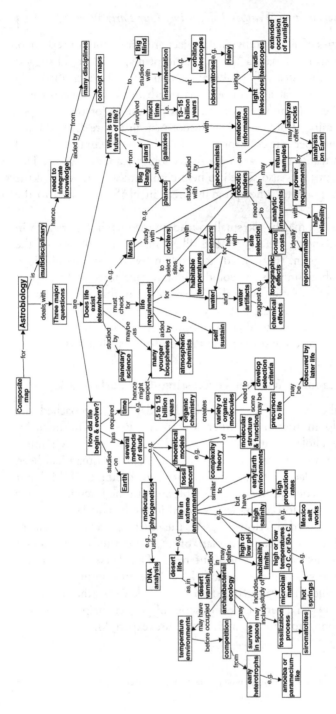

Figure 2.13 A concept map prepared by combining ideas from eight separate research programs that were part of the NASA Astrobiology Program. Part of the concept map from the Archaebacteria Research team is incorporated into the lower left of this concept map.

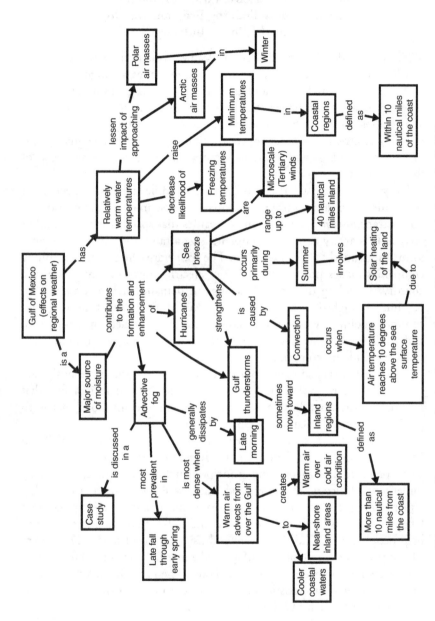

Figure 2.14 Concept map showing the major factors affecting precipitation in the Gulf Coast area.

Understanding Electric Power Production and Transmission: A Training Program Developed for the Power Industry

While our work with the Pensacola weather forecasters was proceeding, IHMC was approached by a company to explore how we might help them improve their research and training programs. This organization represents power generating and power transmission companies in the United States and focuses on research to find more effective methods to produce and transmit electricity. We developed a training program for engineers and managers working with various companies that were members of this consortium.

Early on, I was surprised to learn that while all power generation companies own some power transmission lines, most of them also buy power transmission services from companies that specialize in this kind of service. It is a very complex, comprehensive arrangement that all together forms the United States power grid. The cooperative arrangements among companies makes possible provision of electric power to any part of the country, including during wide swings in demand such as occurs from daytime to nighttime to those that occur during winter heating and summer cooling. Most of the monitoring is controlled by computers, and while there is human oversight, most of the minute-to-minute decisions are made by computers.

Because there are so many companies involved and the relationships are so complex, it is easy to understand why currently there is a fear that terrorists – or other hostile countries – might use insidious means to partially or totally collapse the US power grid.

We conducted a series of three-day training programs at IHMC in Pensacola, Florida (see Figure 2.15). My role was primarily to introduce participants to the theory and principles of learning and epistemology underlying concept mapping and that were also used to develop CmapTools software. In fact, these were the ten rules I introduced in Chapter 1 of this book. Alberto Cañas and I also prepared a document to help people understand the nature and use of concept maps. This paper, "Theory Underlying Concept Maps and How to Construct Them," was later posted on the website for CmapTools. The paper included a concept map describing characteristics of good concept maps shown in Chapter 1. You may want to refer back to Figure 1.10.

Our training was focused on better ways to train new employees and to enhance research on various aspects of power generation and distribution.

Figure 2.15   The author (in sweater at lower right) introducing a team to theory
underlying concept maps. He then began a knowledge elicitation session
with the group.

Therefore, we involved all of the participants in every phase of the
instructional program so that they could lead similar training programs
for staff in their individual companies when they returned home.

For the most part, all the teams were interested to learn about the
theoretical foundations underlying concept mapping. Although
CmapTools appear simple on the surface, they were amazed to discover
how precisely a concept map could capture and present a very complex set
of ideas about power generation and power transmission. I believe many
were also surprised at how quickly they could become proficient in leading
a knowledge elicitation session and at how quickly any participant learned
to build a concept map from the knowledge being elicited and recorded
using CmapTools. The photo in Figure 2.16 shows one of the participants
at the projector screen eliciting the knowledge of an expert and suggesting
how to record it in the developing concept map. A second participant is
using CmapTools to record the concept map as it is being developed and
projected on the screen.

Figure 2.16   A participant is leading this knowledge elicitation session to build a concept map for the group viewed on the screen. Another participant is recording the concept map projected on the screen for the group as the session progresses.

However, I believe some of the products of our work could also be of value in education programs to help the public better understand this important industry. Figure 2.17 is an example of the concept maps prepared by the IHMC team working together with staff of a power company. This concept map contains many additional resources that are included in the files, but these are available only when a person is connected to the IHMC server and is working with the maps while online.

One of the positive outcomes of this training program was an invitation to help with training new engineers at a nuclear power plant. With the virtual thirty-year shutdown in the building of nuclear power plants, most universities have shut down programs for training nuclear power engineers. The result is that most of the currently employed engineers are nearing retirement and companies are having trouble finding replacements. To solve the problem, many plants are developing their own training programs. They are finding that the use of concept maps is very helpful in this training.

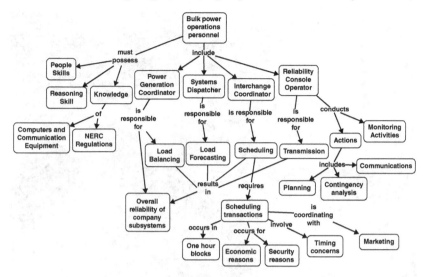

Figure 2.17   A concept map showing the many factors that need to be considered to maintain electricity supply to customers of the power company. After completion of this map, the staff identified eighteen resources that could be accessed via icons at the bottom of concept boxes.

We began our work in 2003 by interviewing senior engineers and preparing concept maps that capture their expertise in a lucid, easily understood manner. Some of the staff sat in with us during these "capturing expert knowledge sessions." We wanted them to learn how to do this kind of expert knowledge capture so that they could develop their own expert knowledge maps as they came to recognize problem areas that needed this kind of training but for which we had not yet prepared concept maps. This would allow management to update their training programs whenever needed.

There are a great many individual components in a nuclear power plant. Each of these must operate in harmony with all the others. While some of the activities of components are controlled by a human operator, most of the minute-to-minute changes are controlled by computers. The control panel shown in Figure 2.18 is a replica of an actual control panel for a nuclear plant, but it only simulates the control functions, much in the same way as simulators are used to train pilots. The facility's program to train new engineers or to upgrade the skills of engineers used this simulator together with training sessions with concept maps and instructors. The panel also allows trainers to modify readings on most of the recorders to

Figure 2.18   The author is studying the training control panel at a nuclear power plant.
This panel is identical to the control panel used for actual control of the power plant.

simulate conditions and problems similar to those that actually occur in
the plant's operation. Thus, the performance of a person being trained can
be "tested" over a wide range of events that may actually occur at some
time in the operation of the plant. Such training, when well done, assures
that the trainee will perform with 100 percent success when they are
working on the functional control panel for the power plant. Of course,
there is also an experienced operator monitoring the performance of the
trainee when they begin work on the actual plant control panel. In some
ways the training is similar to that for new auto drivers or airline pilots,
except there are thousands or even millions of people who can be affected
by a single operator's mistakes.

It has been gratifying to me to see how well the tools and ideas we first
developed to improve teaching and learning in schools and colleges can be
equally effective in the sorts of corporate settings I have described. I know
of no way to put a dollar value on the benefits that derived from our work
with the various companies, but in any case, I am confident it would be
measured in six figures, if not more.

Helping to Keep America Safe

As we were winding down our activities with the power industry, the IHMC was approached by staff from a security organization to conduct a training program for staff members. The training program was in part to assist in coordinating intelligence operations to prevent future terrorist attacks. An analysis of what had gone wrong that led to the 9/11 terrorist attack on the World Trade Center had shown that a major problem was that there was no mechanism for coordination of the various bits of information that are collected. We have had a number of terrorist attacks in the USA since 9/11, but nothing close to the scale of the 2001 attack.

Our first staff training program was held in March 2004 in the classroom of IHMC (see Figure 2.19). There were twenty-two participants, and one participant was selected to serve as the leader for the organization. This participant played an important role in explaining our work to other staff and administrators. He was also instrumental in the future funding of projects. On the first day of our program, I presented a PowerPoint discussion of the key ideas about the nature of knowledge and human learning, and reasons why concept mapping can be effective in new learning and coordinating efforts to better utilize knowledge. Each of the participants prepared one or more concept maps of their own in the training sessions, but because of the proprietary nature of their work, none of these maps dealt with actual events or cases with which the participants had been dealing.

In follow-up conversations with the leader, I shared the concept map in Figure 2.20 to get his comments on whether or not this representation might be useful to help explain how concept maps might be used. He

The Theory and Principles Underlying Concept Mapping and Implications For Educating

Joseph D. Novak

Cornell University and
Institute for Human and Machine Cognition

jnovak@ihmc.us

Figure 2.19   PowerPoint presentation to teach participants to use concept maps for processing secure information: How CmapTools can help staff to "connect the dots."

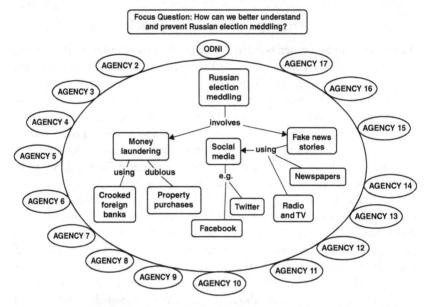

Figure 2.20   A model for the use of CmapTools as an organizing tool for combining information inputs from all agencies charged with preventing Russian meddling in US elections.

informed me that this kind of inquiry is not in his scope of work and explained that there was a group responsible for this work. He said he would try to share this map with that office. In a conversation with the group leader one evening after a training session, I asked him how his organization was using concept maps. He assured me that the use of concept maps has been and continues to be effective in "catching bad guys."

It was never my intention to pursue consulting work aggressively, and I continued to spend the larger fraction of my time doing scholarly writing, participating in research projects, and maintaining my professional ties with various organizations. My post-Cornell University retirement years were very busy, but they were also very rewarding in many ways, including providing some extra income. I especially enjoyed my work with the IHMC in Pensacola. Some of this work was described earlier, and more will be presented in later sections of this book. After knee replacement in 2007 and lower back surgery in 2008, travel became more difficult, and I closed down my formal consulting business. I intend to continue my efforts to help people learn as long as my health permits.

CHAPTER 3

Building a Theory of Education

Can Education Become a Science?

As I observed in Chapter 1, I noticed a striking difference in the courses I took in the College of Education compared with the science courses I had been taking. Both fields of study had notable historical figures, but unlike the notables in science, none of the persons discussed in education courses had produced anything like a theory or a major principle to explain how or why events or objects studied in education behaved the way they do. There was nothing like atomic theory that explains the structure and changes in matter, or Darwin's (1873) theory of evolution that helps to explain why all organisms have similarities in the structures and functions we observe. My undergraduate and graduate studies in psychology did attempt to present some "laws of learning," but these dealt primarily with animal behaviors that had little connection to human learning.

I recognized, of course, that human beings have more control over their destinies than other organisms, but they are still a part of the world of organic life, and there should be some basic rules or principles and maybe even theories that help to explain how and why humans vary so greatly in their success in acquiring and using knowledge. In short, I became committed to the idea that if we want to create revolutionary improvement in education, we needed to seek to build a *science* of education. This science should help us understand why education is often so ineffective and why great teachers achieve the successes we observe.

Even as a child I wondered how people came up with new ideas and created new knowledge. I also wondered about what is this stuff we call knowledge, and are there common things about the nature of knowledge that are similar to "building blocks" in all fields of knowledge? Electrons, protons, and neutrons make up the structure of all atoms, and some 100 kinds of atoms make up the structure of everything we observe in the universe. Is there something like "atoms of knowledge," and if such "atoms of knowledge" exist, what are they? And how are they put together to create the stories and explanations man has constructed over millennia? As I noted in Chapter 1, my undergraduate and graduate courses in psychology, sociology, and educational psychology were essentially useless to my pursuit of understanding the nature of knowledge and how humans create new knowledge.

As a graduate student, I enrolled in a course called "Theories of Learning," taught by Professor Gordon Mork. The textbook used was *Theories of Learning* (Hilgard, 1948). The course dealt almost exclusively with the behavioral psychology of B. F. Skinner and other behavioral psychologists. As the course progressed, I became increasingly frustrated with what I saw as the lack of relevance of the research and ideas presented for finding better ways to teach science so my students would understand the important concepts of science. When I complained to Professor Mork that I thought the course was essentially irrelevant to school education, his response was that Hilgard's book was the most commonly used in graduate educational psychology courses and he knew of no better theories of learning.

There were, of course, Frederic Bartlett's (1932) cognitive schema theory of learning and the writings of Jean Piaget in the 1920s to 1970s, but psychology was so dominated by behaviorists in the 1950s that these *cognitive* theories of learning were simply ignored. I mentioned my conversation with Mork to my colleague Bob Gowin and he said he had the same kind of conversation with his professor of educational psychology at Stanford University. It is one reason I cautioned my graduate students: "Never underestimate the tenacity of stupidity!" Not only do we see this in education and psychology – but especially in politics. President Trump's insistence that climate change is a hoax is as an example of the latter.

What I seek to do in this chapter is to walk you through some of the important studies my graduate students and I did over a span of some thirty-five years in an effort to create a *science of education* with valid principles and culminating in a viable theory of education. The story includes a number of visiting professors from foreign universities who chose to join our group to be part of this effort, and who in many cases continue to extend this work in their home universities today. It is a story about a sustained commitment that eventually brought some striking successes. One of the most important of these was the invention of the concept map tool to represent knowledge, discussed in the previous chapters.

As my research group continued to work with Ausubel's theory of learning, not only did we come to better understand his theory, but we also wanted to find ways to demonstrate its validity to the science education community. The data we were collecting from testing in biology courses at Purdue University showed that key ideas in his theory were validated in the studies we were doing. For example, we found that students who memorized information on sporozoans in a zoology course were just rote learning the information and they lost half of the information within three weeks and essentially all of it within twelve weeks. The information was never incorporated into the related concepts held by these students and had obviously been learned by pure rote learning (Hagerman, 1966).

In another study, we examined the effect of presenting what Ausubel called an *advance organizer* prior to an instructional unit on homeostasis in animals. Advance organizers serve to facilitate meaningful learning by providing a link or *cognitive bridge* between an idea already familiar to the learner and a related new idea to be learned. Students were first presented with the commonly known idea that thermostats in homes regulate temperature. We then provided instruction on homeostasis in animals and mechanisms animals use to regulate body temperature. Students who were first reminded how home thermostats work did significantly better on test items dealing with the concept of homeostasis in animals given several weeks later. The data supported Ausubel's idea of using *advance organizers* to facilitate meaningful learning (Kuhn, 1967; Novak, 1970). The advance organizer principle is probably the most researched principle in Ausubel's theory, but many of these studies have design flaws such as not demonstrating at first that the students understood the advance organizer, or testing for rote recall of information rather than for students' ability to apply the principle in novel settings.

Seeking a Better Work Setting for Building a Theory of Education

When I returned from my sabbatical at Harvard University in the summer of 1966, I was determined to find another position at a university where I could focus on research that would help to construct a viable theory of education. I had been offered a position at the University of Chicago the summer before my sabbatical, but it would have been another joint appointment in the Science Education and Zoology Departments. I would have been working with Joseph Schwab, a person I held in high regard, but I was not confident I could focus on the research I wanted to do. Moreover, I would have lost the opportunity to take a sabbatical leave from Purdue University and work for nine months at Harvard University.

There are always trade-offs in pursuing career alternatives, and this time I think I again made the right choice.

At Harvard University during 1965–1966, I had almost full time to pursue the kind of research I wanted to do. I also sat on an advisory board guiding the development of a new kind of high school physics course called Harvard Project Physics (HPP). In addition to working with some top Harvard physics professors on this project, I had opportunities to suggest how some of the work we had done in teaching innovations in biology might be applied to the HPP course. I also had time to sit in on some of Jerome Bruner's seminars on cognitive psychology, a pioneering program at the time. Harvard also provided me with a graduate student research assistant and a technician to help with some of the chores associated with our research program.

As I indicated in Chapter 1, I had begun to develop A-T science lessons at Purdue University, but at Harvard I had almost full time to work on new lessons and to find ways to evaluate students' learning from these lessons. We succeeded in developing several lessons dealing with plant growth and several dealing with the nature of electricity. It was evident from interviews we did with students taking our lessons that they were beginning to understand the basic science concepts presented in these lessons, but we needed a better evaluation method to present convincing evidence of their learning.

When I returned to Purdue University in the summer of 1966, my graduate students and I began creating additional new A-T lessons and testing these in local schools. It was difficult to find funding for our work, so progress was slow.

In the winter of 1967, I was invited to apply for a position in science education at Cornell University. My principal work there would be to build a world-class science education program, exactly what I was seeking to do at Purdue University, but without many competing assignments. I began my 28-year career at Cornell University in the fall of 1967.

Building a Research Team at Cornell University

My first course offering at Cornell University was "Theory and Methods of Education." In this course I presented Ausubel's Assimilation Theory of Learning. I also contrasted traditional positivist epistemology with emerging views on the nature of knowledge and knowledge creation. These ideas were new to students who had been in residence for a year or more before I arrived at Cornell. After we developed concept mapping in the early

1970s, I also required my students to design and conduct clinical interviews, and to prepare concept maps from each interview record, as discussed in Chapter 1. My Theory and Methods of Education course became the foundation for new students entering graduate studies with me. Some of the "old" students who had been in residence for a year or more before I arrived became interested in my work, and some "old" students immediately sought to incorporate these new ideas into their ongoing thesis research.

One of these "old" students who became interested in my work was Pinchas Tamir (see Figure 3.1). Pinchas was comparing the performance of biology students in freshman college who had taken one of the newer high school BSCS biology courses with the performance of students who had taken a more traditional high school biology course. Pinchas found significant differences in the performance of these two groups on college biology exams, but he was at a loss to explain why. When he learned about Ausubel's learning theory, he immediately saw that students who had taken BSCS biology had acquired through more *meaningful learning* an understanding of some basic biology concepts emphasized in the BSCS courses. These concepts functioned to anchor new information and new concepts and ideas presented in college biology. He incorporated Ausubel's ideas into his Ph.D. thesis and subsequent research studies and publications. Pinchas took a position in science education at Hebrew University in Israel, where he remained for his entire productive career.

Pinchas visited Cornell University several times after he completed his Ph.D. degree, and he also arranged for me to participate in conferences

Figure 3.1   Pinchas Tamir (1928–2016) was one of the author's first students at Cornell University. He became an international leader in science education.

dealing with ways to improve science education that were held in Israel. We remained close friends until he died from Parkinson's disease. He was a strong advocate for my research work.

Early in my career, I became very active in the National Association for Research in Science Teaching (NARST). This organization, founded in 1918, had a long history of sponsoring meetings where science education scholars presented their research. NARST also sponsored a publication, *Science Education,* that published research relevant to improving science education. There were no comparable organizations in other fields of education at the time, although similar organizations were formed later. From my earliest association with NARST, I sought to promote stronger efforts to build theoretical foundations for science education and education in general.

The journal, *Science Education,* was owned by Clarence Pruitt of the University of Tampa. Pruitt also served as editor, and he did not always adhere to high standards in selecting papers for the publication. When I was elected to membership in NARST in 1978, I joined with leaders of the organization to launch a new journal that would have a more rigorous editorial policy. After a series of negotiations, NARST arranged with John Wiley & Sons Company to publish a new journal in 1963.

The first volume of the new *Journal of Research in Science Teaching* was published in 1963. The editor of the journal invited me to prepare a statement for the first issue that might provide guidance to researchers for improving the quality of research in science education (Novak, 1963). My statement stressed the need for using theory to guide research, whether the work involved surveys of practices, experimental studies or other forms of research.

My statement also stressed the need to seek better theory to guide research in science education. This statement was written before we had discovered Ausubel's 1963 Assimilation Theory of Learning. His theory of learning became an important part of all my future efforts to build a viable theory of education.

As noted in Chapter 1, my research group also sought to develop a better understanding of the nature of knowledge and the process of knowledge creation. Since this was an area of research that my colleague Bob Gowin was also working on, my students benefitted from his classes and discussions.

I was also particularly impressed with the early writings of James Conant in 1948, and later with one of his protégés, Thomas Kuhn. Kuhn's (1962) book, *The Structure of Scientific Revolutions,* described in some detail how paradigms that guide scientific research shift over time. These books often entered into our conversations. We also discussed the work of Stephen Toulmin and his 1972 book, *Human Understanding*, Volume I: *The Collective Use and Evolution of Concepts*. His ideas on the "evolution of concepts" made a lot of sense to me, perhaps in part because of my training as a biologist. They also connected well with Ausubel's ideas of *progressive differentiation* of concepts over a span of new learning. A key idea in Ausubel's learning theory is that as meaningful learning progresses, the learner's basic concepts become modified and clarified over time.

My research group and I became increasingly convinced that Ausubel's learning theory could be very useful for improving research in science education and also for designing better educational practices. We decided to check out Ausubel's theory by using it as a lens to review 156 research studies published by other workers. We sought to ascertain whether or not the results of their work were consistent with what we should expect if we look at the results from the perspective of Ausubel's learning theory. Two of my former students, Donald Ring and Pinchas Tamir, worked with me to review the 156 published research studies. Our goal was to assess whether the findings in these studies would show results that would be expected – if viewed through the lens of Ausubellian learning theory. Most of the studies we found were not based on any learning theory, some had applied ideas from Piagetian theory, and a few were based on behavioral psychology.

It was interesting to us that all the studies we reviewed could have been better designed if they had been guided by Ausubellian theory. In a number of cases, the study results did not support the theory on which they were designed, or the study results could be better explained by applying Ausubellian theory. Our paper was published in 1971 (Novak, Ring, and Tamir, 1971).

We received essentially no comment from any of the authors of the papers we reviewed. Is it any wonder that there has been so little improvement in educational practice as a result of "scholarly" research on teaching and learning? Most educational research simply has no impact on teaching and learning in schools. However, there has been progress in educational research, and I shall present some of this in later sections of this book.

Another one of my first Ph.D. students at Cornell University was Joseph Nussbaum. He had done his MS degree in Israel with Pinchas Tamir, who had recommended he enroll at Cornell University to study with my group. Nussbaum was interested in studying how grade 2 children come to understand the nature of Earth's gravity and its effects on objects. Yossi, as we all came to call Joseph by his Jewish name, developed six A-T lessons that were very effective in presenting ideas to grade 2 children dealing with how gravity acts on objects and the relationship between gravitational force and the planet Earth. As was true with all of the Audio-tutorial lessons we developed, Yossi's lessons underwent a number of revisions before they could work effectively with children in any grade 2 classroom without teacher involvement. Yossi's six lessons were offered as lessons 11 through 16 in our Audio-tutorial program conducted in Ithaca Public Schools in 1971–1973.

After children completed this series of lessons, Yossi interviewed the students to discern what valid or invalid concepts they had developed. Yossi also interviewed grade 2 children in the same schools who did not take the Audio-tutorial lessons. Figure 3.2 shows Yossi interviewing a student using a globe and other materials that were presented in the Audio-tutorial lessons.

Some of the questions Yossi asked in his interviews used a small doll holding a ball. He positioned the doll at various places on the globe and asked: "If this doll were a person standing on the Earth, where would the ball fall?" Yossi also asked where the ball would fall if there was a hole

Figure 3.2 Yossi Nussbaum interviewing a grade 2 child on ideas about Earth and gravity.

drilled through the center of Earth? He also used other questions to ascertain if the child had a concept of the Earth as an object in space.

Yossi found wide variation in the students' understanding of Earth and gravity. He also found that the children's answers could be grouped into five different "notions." Figure 3.3 shows the five different "notions" that he identified. Some of the children could not relate the dropped ball to the "Earth" represented by the globe, and he classified these as children holding Notion 1. Some of the children were aware of the fact that the globe represented the planet Earth, but still thought a ball dropped on this "Earth" would fall to the ground (or to the floor of the room). This he called Notion 2. Another group of students believe the Earth is moving in space, but they thought that if we drop a ball or some water from a bottle it will fall into an ocean or into space. This group he labeled as holding Notion 3. Students he labeled holding Notion 4 know that the Earth is floating in space, and that things we drop will fall toward Earth (i.e., the globe). However, they do not believe that water poured out of a bottle would head toward the center of Earth. Finally, students who held Notion 5 know the Earth floats in space and if we drop anything on the surface it will fall toward the center of the earth. In fact, when shown a drawing of a man dropping an object into a hole through the center of Earth, they say it would fall into the hole and then stop in the center of Earth. These five different notions held by the grade 2 students after instruction are illustrated in Figure 3.3. Nussbaum's study was published in 1976 (Nussbaum and Novak, 1976).

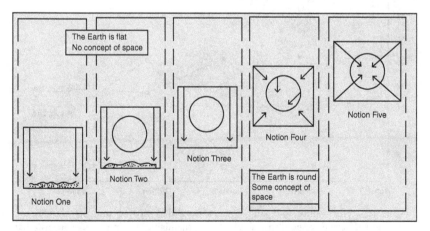

Figure 3.3   Nussbaum's classifications of children's notions of Earth and gravity, 1976.

In a later research study, Nussbaum used the same A-T lesson with grade 6 students. He interviewed samples of these students and also similar samples of grade 2 and grade 6 students who did not have the A-T lessons. He compared the performance of both his instructed and his uninstructed grade 2 and grade 6 children with a sample of grade 4 children in a study done by Mali (1979) in Nepal (see Figure 3.4). Results from Nussbaum's and Mali's studies were combined in a paper published in 1983.

Nussbaum's studies and many others done by members of our research group, or who did research with Nussbaum in Israel, clearly supported the validity of Ausubel's Assimilation Theory of Learning and refuted the validity of Piaget's theory that maintained that children below the age of twelve to fourteen years cannot learn abstract ideas, such as the nature of the effect of Earth's gravity on objects that were dropped. Our research results were consistent with some of the work of early cognitive psychologists such as Donaldson (1978) and Chi (1983).

Although our group was constantly short on funding, I did manage to find support for the research work of more than 200 graduate students during my career. I had very good relationships with all of the science departments and the mathematics department at Cornell. Since most of

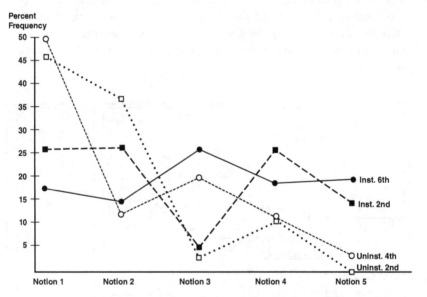

Figure 3.4   Nussbaum's 1983 study graph showed that very few students who did not have the A-T lessons responded with answers in the highest two notions. Note also that grade 2 instructed students did about as well as grade 6 instructed students.

my students had BS or MS degrees in science or mathematics, and most had teaching experience, it was possible to obtain teaching assistantships for these students in a science department or the Mathematics departments. Some of my students were on sabbatical leave from their home institutions in various countries. A small group had scholarships from their home countries. Nussbaum was in this group.

In recent years there have been a number of reports in newspapers and social media on the shocking lack of understanding of the shape of planet Earth held by teenagers and adults in the USA and other countries. Although percentages reported vary from report to report, most of these reports indicate that some 15 to 40 percent of adults believe that the earth is flat like a pancake and that you could fall into space if you wander to the edge of the earth. These high percentages of adults who hold invalid ideas about the shape of planet Earth and its position in space are evidence of the shocking failure of science education in the USA. The past two decades of "No Child Left Behind" programs in the USA illustrate the failure of instructional programs that center on memorizing information to pass multiple-choice tests now widely employed in schools. In later chapters I will discuss more promising alternatives.

Building a Solid Epistemological Foundation

I discussed briefly in Chapter 1 and earlier in this chapter my efforts to jettison what I saw as the curse of logical positivism. Even as a graduate student I saw the relationship between understanding the nature of human learning and the nature of new knowledge creation as inseparably bound together. Several of my graduate students became interested in exploring the relationships that might be found between Ausubel's Assimilation Learning Theory and the emerging constuctivist epistemology. One of my exceptional students, Barbara Bowen, decided to explore better theoretical foundations for education in her 1972 Ph.D. thesis work. Barbara was involved in the feminist movement of the 1960s and she was deeply troubled by what she saw as rampant sexual bias in most institutions. I valued her efforts to fight sexual, racist, and elitist biases. Barbara showed in her thesis that we could find close relationships between Ausubel's and Toulmin's ideas, and this advanced my thinking on how epistemological ideas could serve to help us help people understand key ideas in Ausubel's learning theory and the emerging constructivist epistemology. For example, Ausubel's principle of *progressive differentiation* says that as a learner acquires new, relevant information using meaningful learning, that information is subsumed into her/his relevant anchoring concept. Both the new concept and the anchoring concept become somewhat modified over time. This process also describes the process by which concept meanings evolve over time, as Kuhn (1962) describes in his epistemological views on the nature of knowledge and conceptual paradigm change over time. Barbara described a number of such parallels in Ausubel's learning theory and Toulmin and other philosophers' views on epistemology.

More than any other of my graduate students, Barbara recognized the petty politics that often prevail in academia and she was not interested in entering that game after she completed her doctorate. She had a successful career with Apple Corporation helping to adapt emerging technologies to address problems in education. She also was successful in doing consulting work with schools, corporations, and other organizations. From the time of completion of her Ph.D. thesis until her unfortunate death in 2016, Barbara helped me learn.

The late 1960s were turbulent times on the Cornell University campus, and many other campuses. There were numerous demonstrations against the Vietnam war, and for Black rights, gay and lesbian rights, and woman's rights. At one point, militant Black students took over a house on the edge of the Cornell campus where we had my research projects housed, and we had to make a hasty Sunday morning move to temporary space in the old Physics building. Some of my students were involved in some of these demonstrations, and in general, I supported the causes they pursued as long as the actions did not result in personal injuries or property destruction. I was hopeful that the various protests would result in positive social changes, and at least to some extent, this did occur. I also hoped we might not see again the USA engaged in what I saw as a foolish war, but then we pushed into what I saw as another foolish war in Iraq in the early 2000s.

A First Effort to Build a Theory of Education

As our research work progressed at Cornell University, we sought to test the validity of the key ideas in Ausubel's learning theory. Studies such as Nussbaum's and many others done by our groups all supported the validity of key ideas of Ausubel's learning theory. Mentioned earlier was our analysis of 156 published research studies done by others which had not considered using Ausubel's learning theory. However, our findings showed that their results would have been best explained had they used Ausubel's learning theory.

Our studies also showed the important role that feelings play in meaningful learning. For example, in selecting materials to use in our Audio-tutorial lesson, we sought not only to use activities and objects that would help students learn a certain concept but also to use examples that students found fun to do or interesting to observe to futher encourge them to engage in meaningful learning of the target concept or concepts being illustrated.

Mauritz Johnson (1967), one of my colleagues at Cornell, had proposed a model for curriculum theory and design of instruction that specified desired instructional outcomes and assessment to determine the extent to which these outcomes are achieved. I incorporated Johnson's ideas into my theory of education by identifying the concepts and propositions we desired our students to learn and understand. Interviews and other assessment strategies could be used to ascertain the extent to which we succeeded in achieving the desired learning outcomes.

In 1973–1974, I was struggling to find a solid epistemological foundation for my theory when I learned of Toulmin's recent book, *Human Understanding*, Volume 1: *The Collective Use and Evolution of Concepts*. Although I learned later in conversations with Toulmin that he was not familiar with Ausubel's learning theory, I saw Toulmin's ideas on the evolution of concepts in a discipline as closely related to Ausubel's ideas of progressive *differentiation* as a learner acquired new subordinate or related concepts in the process of meaningful learning. The 1972 Ph.D. thesis work of my graduate student Barbara Bowen, which I mentioned earlier, helped me shape my ideas on the nature of knowledge and knowledge creation.

Toulmin's ideas on epistemology helped me integrate Ausubel's learning theory and Johnson's theory of curriculm and instruction into what I thought was a good first effort to put forward a theory of education. My book was published by Cornell University Press in 1977 (see Figure 3.5). Ralph W. Tyler, an internationally distinguished educator, wrote a very complimentary Foreword, and I was hopeful that my theory would have a positive impact on the field of education. I did have a one-hour interview on a nationally televised program, *Ask Washington*, in 1978, and the book was translated into Spanish, Portuguese, and Basque. Although I still get notices about once a month that the book has been cited by other scholars, it is evident that this pioneering effort to create a science of education has had only modest success at best.

Although the world of education was not ready to embrace any comprehensive theory of education in 1977, the book and our work did attract the attention of many leaders in science education, and I began to have a

Figure 3.5   The author's first effort to put forward a theory of education was published by Cornell University Press in 1977.

steady stream of international visitors and visiting professors every year. We continued to struggle to obtain enough funding for our work, even though the National Science Foundation had begun to provide multi-million dollar grants to curriculum development programs at other universities, most of them based on Piaget's ideas of learning and cognitive development or on behavioral psychology. While most of these programs were successful in updating the science and math content, few succeeded in changing pedagogical pactices. Most classes continued to be teacher led, a chapter-by-chapter journey through the book and laboratory guide.

During the 1970s, there was a growing recognition that the emerging views of knowledge and nature of knowledge creation were moving away from positivist and logical positivist ideas toward the view that knowledge is a human construction. Positivism and logical positivism were put forth by very capable people such as Auguste Compte in the nineteenth century and Karl Popper in the twentieth century (Popper 1959, 1982). Their view was that through rigorous research we can discover laws of nature that would be true and valid forever. Although these views are losing favor, they remain, often subtly, in many current works in psychology and education.

My colleague at Cornell University, Bob Gowin, had done his Ph.D. studies in the area of philosophy of education. My students and I found his ideas refreshing, and we often did seminars together. Gowin invented a heuristic device we came to call Gowin's Vee, or the Knowledge Vee. Gowin identified twelve "elements" that function in the construction of new knowledge, and he showed the relationships of these elements in a Vee diagram. The twelve elements and their relationships are shown below in Figure 3.6.

Each element on the left side interacts with each element on the right side in the process of constructing new knowledge claims about events or objects in the universe. What is amazing is that the process of knowledge creation shown in the Vee can be applied to creative thinking in any field, from science and engineering to music and literature. We provided examples from many of these fields in our 1984 book, *Learning How to Learn*. I suggest that you pause your reading at this point and try to create one of your own Vee diagrams for some question or creation you are interested in exploring.

Building a Human Constructivist View of Epistemology

In contrast to the positivists, the view of Conant, Kuhn, Toulmin, and others held that the goal of research and innovation was not to find new,

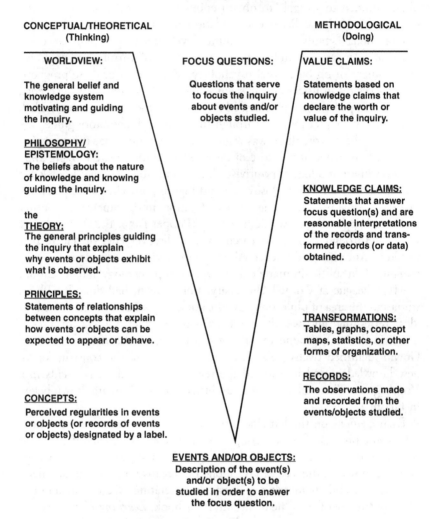

THE KNOWLEDGE VEE

CONCEPTUAL/THEORETICAL
(Thinking)

METHODOLOGICAL
(Doing)

WORLDVIEW:

The general belief and
knowledge system
motivating and guiding
the inquiry.

PHILOSOPHY/
EPISTEMOLOGY:
The beliefs about the nature
of knowledge and knowing
guiding the inquiry.

the
THEORY:
The general principles guiding
the inquiry that explain
why events or objects exhibit
what is observed.

PRINCIPLES:
Statements of relationships
between concepts that explain
how events or objects can be
expected to appear or behave.

CONCEPTS:
Perceived regularities in events
or objects (or records of events
or objects) designated by a label.

FOCUS QUESTIONS:

Questions that serve
to focus the inquiry
about events and/or
objects studied.

VALUE CLAIMS:

Statements based on
knowledge claims that
declare the worth or
value of the inquiry.

KNOWLEDGE CLAIMS:
Statements that answer
focus question(s) and are
reasonable interpretations
of the records and trans-
formed records (or data)
obtained.

TRANSFORMATIONS:
Tables, graphs, concept
maps, statistics, or other
forms of organization.

RECORDS:
The observations made
and recorded from the
events/objects studied.

EVENTS AND/OR OBJECTS:
Description of the event(s)
and/or object(s) to be
studied in order to answer
the focus question.

Figure 3.6   Gowin's Vee heuristic showing the twelve epistemological elements involved
in new knowledge creation. All elements interact with each other in the process of
knowledge creation.

immutable "laws," but rather to search for better explanatory frameworks.
This process continues forever, and the search has no end. Instead of
immutable laws, the search leads to better, more robust explanatory
models. This view came to be known as *constuctivism*, and this became

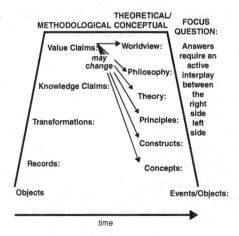

Figure 3.7   The Parade of Vees illustrating the constructivist view that we build on
prior knowledge to create new knowledge, and this is a continuous process.
Some elements are omitted to simplify the figure.

the dominant epistemological view by the late 1990s. Figure 3.7 employs
Gowin's Knowledge Vee to illustrate the evolving process of knowledge
creation. As noted earlier, all twelve elements on the Vee interact in the
process of knowledge creation. New Value Claims and Knowledge Claims
feed into guiding the next inquiry – and the parade of inquiry goes on
and on.

The 1980s and 1990s were remarkable decades in many ways. In the
world of psychology, there was an accelerating movement toward cognitive
psychology, with research efforts centering on understanding how the
brain acquires, stores, and uses knowledge. In the world of epistemology,
there was almost a universal move toward "constructivist" views of knowledge and knowledge creation. One of the persons widely associated with
this movement away from positivism and toward constructivism was Ernst
von Glasersfeld (1984). His writing presented his idea of *radical constructivism.* Not only did von Glasersfeld reject the positivist view of the goal of
finding enduring explanatory "laws," but he held that we can never find
such laws. Our explanatory ideas will always be imperfect and modifiied
over time (von Glasersfeld, 1984).

In addition to Bowen, two other of my graduate students contributed to
my thinking about epistemology and a viable theory of education. Rick
Iuli and Kathy Edmondson both chose to focus on epistemology in their
Ph.D. thesis work and we subsequently coauthored papers on this work

(Edmondson and Novak, 1993; Novak and Iuli, 1995). Kathy also contributed a chapter to a book I coedited in 2004, "Assessing Science Understanding through Concept Maps" (2004).

In 1993, I put forward an epistemology I called *human constuctivism*. Humans think, feel, and act. *Human constructivism* builds on Ausubel's theory of learning, especially his idea that only meaningful learning results in the acquisition, development, and elaboration of new ideas. I further argue that creative thinking is primarily the result of very high levels of meaningful learning. Human thinking is also strongly driven by our feelings or our *affective* domain. What drives an individual to sustain an effort to better understand an idea or event is her/his emotional commitment.

To understand creativity, one must seek to understand deeply the process of meaningful learning. I have found this to be a lifelong endeavor. We begin with the idea that meaningful learning involves integrating a new subordinate idea into a more general, more inclusive superordinate concept. In this process, both the meaning of the subsumed concept and the meaning of the superordinante concept become somewhat modified. Ausubel symbolized this as: A+a becomes A'a'. Further meaningful learning in a knowledge domain may result in: B+b becoming B'b'. Continued meaningful learning may result in what Ausubel calls *superordinate* learning, where two or more subordinate ideas are integrated into the meaning of a new, more inclusive concept. We can show this as: C + A'a' + B'b' leads to C'A"a"B"b". In other words, in superordinate learning, both the more gerneral, more inclusive idea C and the more specific ideas (A' and B') all become slightly modified and refined. The superiority of meaningful learning over rote learning is that only meaningful learning leads to highly integrated, richly interrelated conceptual frameworks. Only meaningful learning allows a person to see the "big pictures" of any domain of knowledge. For example, this was illustrated in the work of Nussbaum cited earlier. Children need to build an understanding of Earth, gravity, space, and motion, and come to see these as a related whole system. Helping researchers see the "big picture" for research in astrobiology was one of the goals of the NASA program described in the last chapter.

The 1980s also saw the invention of personal computers and the World Wide Web. Both of these innovations have had a profound influence on how humans invent, access, organize, and use knowledge. Some of these innovations were presented earlier, and more will be discussed in later chapters.

In the last decade, neurobiologists have discovered that our brains contain special nerve cells that actually represent physical space in our brains and may organize our conceptual forms of knowledge. These cells have been called *grid* cells, and the functions of these cells are now being vigoroulsy pursued using superior functional Magnetic Resonance Imaging (fMRI). The new fMRI machines are vastly superior to the machine that Bruce Dunn had assembled in his lab in the 1980s. The machine we used then made limited surface brain recordings from twenty-one electrode sites (see Figure 2.1). Modern fMRI machines can gather information from essentially the whole brain. While this research is still in its infancy, findings already support Ausubel's ideas on the subsumptive and superordinate organization of knowledge that results from meaningful learning (Underwood, 2015).

We have found in our work that for any domain of knowledge, there may be 20 to 100 or more major concepts involved in understanding that domain. Only meaningful learning can lead to understanding how those many concepts "fit together." In later chapters I will continue to illustrate with more examples how we and others have used concept mapping to help people learn in any domain of knowledge and to better organize and integrate their conceptual understanding of that domain. In case after case, we have seen creative solutions emerge for individuals and teams working on problems in their field. This was illustrated in the work of Christi Palmer's research on prevention of gray mold. This is why meaningful learning is such a profound process – and why concept mapping can be so helpful in new learning in any domain. This is also why having the emotional drive to sustain the process of new knowledge creation is so essential. Figure 3.8 illustrates my view of human constructivism, the process by which humans create new knowledge.

I first published my human constructivism theory of knowledge and knowledge creation in 1983. This became the epistemology my team worked with at Cornell University until I retired in 1995. A slightly updated version was published in 1993. For my research team at Cornell and for most of the work I have done since, including collaborations with IHMC, this view of knowledge and knowledge creation proved to be as useful in work with corporations and governmental and other organizations as in all levels of formal education.

A Theory of Curriculum and Instruction

To be comprehensive, a theory of education must involve: 1. A theory of learning, 2. a theory of knowledge or epistemology, and 3. a theory of curriculum and instruction. I mentioned earlier in this chapter Mauritz

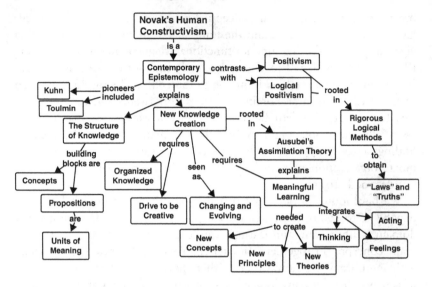

Figure 3.8   Human constructivism is an epistemology, based in part on Ausubel's Assimilation Theory of Learning, which recognizes the constructive interplay of human thinking, feeling, and acting.

Johnson's theory of curriculum and instruction. While Johnson's ideas were helpful to our research team in the early days of our work, we found them less useful as we moved forward on the incorporation of Ausubel's Assimilation Theory of Learning and newer epistemological ideas that became central to our work.

In 1973, Schwab proposed a model for curriculum that presented four "commonplaces" that must be considered in education: learner, teacher, subject matter, and social matrix. I saw value in his ideas. Schwab's ideas made a career move to the University of Chicago attractive to me in 1965, as noted earlier. As we worked with Schwab's ideas, we also found these four commonplaces to be essential in the design and execution of a sound education program. However, we also saw that the kind of testing or evaluation program used can have a profound effect on teachers and learners and preferred to separate this from Schwab's social matrix commonplace. We also chose to call these four components of education "elements," instead of commonplaces. Furthermore, we found the more general term of context to be better to represent the idea of the environment in which education takes place. Nevertheless, we agreed with Schwab that all of these elements need to be considered.

In the design of an optimal education program, all four elements must be designed so as to optimize meaningful learning. I first illustrated how this may be done effectively in my book *Learning, Creating and Using Knowledge: Concept maps as facilitating tools in schools and corporations* (Novak, 1998).

Putting It All Together into a Coherent Theory of Education

From the perspective of my research team, we have succeeded in building a coherent theory of education that is sufficiently comprehensive to guide the improvement of education in any discipline, at any age level, and in any setting. Some examples of this work will be presented in later chapters. The theory incorporates all five elements involved in education and places emphasis on meaningful learning. It also recognizes that human thinking, feeling, and acting are all involved in learning. When all of these factors are well integrated in learning, the learner not only succeeds in building understandings but also feels empowered and committed to positive social change. This view of the theory is represented in the Figure 3.9.

It is exciting to imagine what societies would be like if great education were available to all citizens in every country. Needless to say, dictatorships and countries with despotic rulers will do everything necessary to prevent this. The challenge we face is how to improve education for the masses wherever this is possible. The theory and program for this was further elaborated in a second edition of *Learning, Creating, and Using Knowledge* (see Figure 3.10). The latter book sought to further document and advance those ideas. Translations of the first or second editions were published in Chinese, Finnish, Italian, Portuguese, and Spanish.

Over the years, I have come to appreciate the profound meaning of the concept meaningful learning. The more my students, collaborators, and I have sought to apply this concept in new contexts, the more we see new ways in which the concept confers new meaning and new explanatory power to some problem or issue we are dealing with. As a biologist, I like to compare the explanatory power of meaningful learning in education to the explanatory power of the concept of evolution in biology. The concept of evolution helps us understand everything, from how viruses mutate and how to develop new drugs to deal with new viruses, to changes that are occurring in the planet's ecosystems as a result of climate change. This is why the idea of meaningful learning plays such a central role in my theory of education. Einstein's special theory of relativity can be summarized as: Energy equals mass times the square of the velocity of light in centimeters

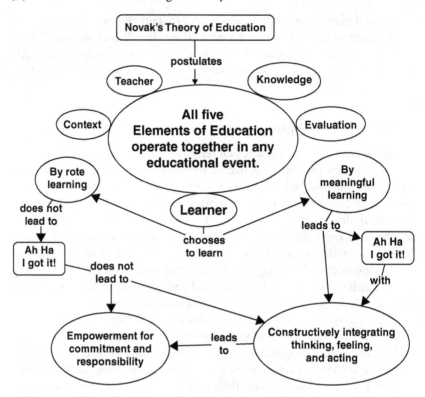

Figure 3.9 The author's theory of education integrates all five elements involved in education through effective meaningful learning and leads to learners empowered for high levels of commitment and responsibility.

(E=MC²). My theory of education can be summarized, less elegantly, as shown in Figure 3.11.

As we progress through the remaining chapters of this book, refer back to this statement and judge for yourself if it helps to clarify and elucidate solutions for helping people learn.

Theories Need to be Tested

Earlier in this chapter I described how two of my former graduate students and I used published literature in science education to test if Ausubel's learning theory could predict the results reported in research studies in science education done by other researchers, none of whom used Ausubel's theory to guide their work. Ausubel's theory not only could have predicted better the results obtained but would also have suggested ways that the

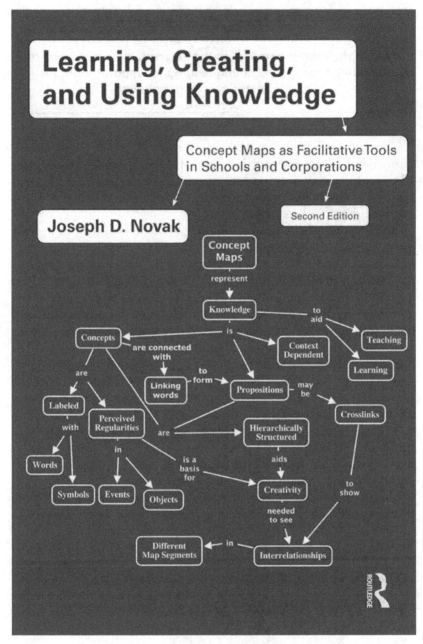

Figure 3.10   The author presents his latest comprehensive view of his theory of education and suggestions for implementing the ideas into practice in any educational or management setting (Novak, 2010).

A Theory of Education

Meaningful learning underlies the constructive integration of thinking, feeling, and acting leading to empowerment for commitment and responsibility.
J. Novak

Figure 3.11   The author's theory of education summarized as a single statement.

instructional programs could have been improved to make them more effective. Of course, we also built on thirty years of our own research studies and educational innovations that were based on Ausubel's theory and were shown to be effective.

In the course of our research program, we found it useful to devise a questionnaire that would quickly ascertain a person's views on the nature of knowledge and the nature of learning. Earlier versions of the questionnaire contain thirty to forty items, but we later found that we could get reasonably reliable classifications of students with a much shorter Learning Strategies Questionnaire with just seventeen items. This questionnaire is presented in Appendix 1. I suggest that you identify a group of thirty or more willing participants and administer this questionnaire to them. The questionnaire also provides for obtaining information on participants' voting records and their schooling. My theory would predict that the participants with the best voting records would also be most inclined toward meaningful learning.

You may wish to design your own research study to test key aspects of my theory. For example, are schools that place emphasis on learning for understanding also helping their students to become more responsible citizens in their community? I will present, in Chapter 5, results from one recent study that suggests this may be the case. Testing theories of education will lead not only to better education but to better societies.

Surprising Comment from David Ausubel on My Work

In our early work with A-T lessons, we used Ausubel's ideas to guide our work as we developed lesson scripts and selected hands-on learning activities to include in the lessons. I invited David to visit our program on several occasions, and he took the time needed to observe children working with lessons in school settings. He also looked at some of the interviews that were done and the data we were collecting to demonstrate that the children were acquiring an understanding of the basic science concepts we were teaching. Unlike many other competent visitors we had observing our work, David was characteristically silent or very modest with his compliments. This was also the case when I sent him copies of our research papers as they began to emerge.

After my retirement from Cornell University in 1995, several of my former graduate students and other colleagues organized the Fifth International Seminar on Research Studies on Misconceptions in Science and Mathematics Education. This seminar was also used as an opportunity to recognize and celebrate the research achievements of my group. A special dinner was held in my honor and participants were asked to submit a letter to the Conference chairperson expressing their thoughts and feelings about the research work we had been doing for over thirty years. Some seventy letters were submitted, and they were all highly complementary. The letter from David most surprised me. He commented:

> In my opinion, this work by Joseph Novak is without any doubt the most significant and unparallelly original psychological and educational research performed in this basic area of educational psychology during the past 3+ decades – not only because it provided sorely-needed empirical substantiation for theoretical postulates regarding the nature of cognitive processes underlying the acquisition and retention of knowledges, but also because it added substantially to our understanding (with built-in empirical verification) of how these processes function and are mediated.

Although I did not receive this letter from Ausubel until Kathy Edmondson visited me in January of 2020, it was still very gratifying to learn that he held my work in such high regard. I only wish he were still alive so that I could express my appreciation for this letter.

CHAPTER 4

The Design of Better Instructional Programs

A Study of Exemplary School Science Facilities and Programs

In 1969, I was asked to direct a study of exemplary secondary school science facilities and programs in United States schools. The study was proposed by the National Science Teachers Association (NSTA) and funded by the National Science Foundation (NSF). I was surprised to learn that an earlier proposal with other leadership was rejected by NSF, but they indicated they might fund the project if I agreed to lead it. The reason this surprised me is that for several years, the leadership at NSF had refused to fund any of my research proposals, primarily because they rejected the theoretical foundations of my research program.

A study team composed of six respected science educators who would assist me in forming the criteria for judging the school facilities and programs and doing site visitations to schools were selected. An advisory board of twelve senior school leaders, scientists, and science educators provided some guidance as the study planning and program progressed.

We began by soliciting nominations of schools that had outstanding science facilities and/or science programs. NSTA had many national contacts with equipment supply companies, science book representatives, and science education leaders in all states. We sent out requests for nominations along with the criteria we had so far identified as indicators of exemplary facilities and/or instructional programs. We received over 600 nominations. Through phone calls and a few visitations to schools, the study group found that there was great variation in the schools nominated and that most were not truly exemplary in their facilities or instructional programs. In the end, we selected and visited 160 schools, some of them on more than one occasion. A few thousand photos and many pages of notes were taken by study team members.

Study team members met periodically over the course of the study to share what they were finding and to discuss what we called *evolving patterns* in facilities and programs. The idea of evolving patterns derived from our observations of facilities and programs and our conversations with teachers and administrators. Staff members discussed the limitations of prior facilities or programs and their reasons for making the changes to those that we observed. After much discussion, we identified four evolving patterns. Each pattern progressed from "older" facilities or programs to what our committee judged to be the most forward looking. In the end, we identified four *evolving patterns.*

The first pattern identified dealt with changing physical facilities, moving from thirty-student classrooms with laboratory tables at the periphery or in the back of the room (most common) to large open areas with movable lab tables and a central laboratory supply room and adjacent individual project rooms. The second pattern dealt with evolving patterns in the use of technology. Here we observed the use of blackboards or overhead projectors to centrally located TV equipped study carrels, to use audiovisual aids primarily by student teams for reporting on their work. The third pattern dealt with instructional programs, from the traditional chapter-by-chapter discussion of text information and little laboratory work to student teams working on assignments and team project work. Finally, but perhaps most important, we observed student–staff interactions as moving from teacher lectures, weekly quizzes, and multiple-choice group testing, to heterogeneous age grouping for project work and individualized evaluation. Figure 4.1 shows the key features of these four "evolving patterns" we identified.

We observed some new facilities that were probably more of a publicity stunt by the administration than a creative modification to improve teaching and learning. For example, the idea of "open classrooms" became popular in some British schools in the 1940s, and this idea was brought to some American schools in the 1950s. The idea was to allow more cross-age study and interdisciplinary study by providing large spaces for study and project work. However, without retraining teachers and redesigning instruction, these "open classrooms" became a nuisance, and teachers soon found ways to arrange bookcases and other barriers to return closer to the traditional classroom in spaces and instructional programs.

Another school we observed had built a large room with 100 or so study carrels with dial access television available in each carrel. The only activity our team observed was students listening to music or simply using the carrel to study traditional lessons. Without training teachers to work with students to develop useful television learning experiences, this facility was seldom used for actual instruction.

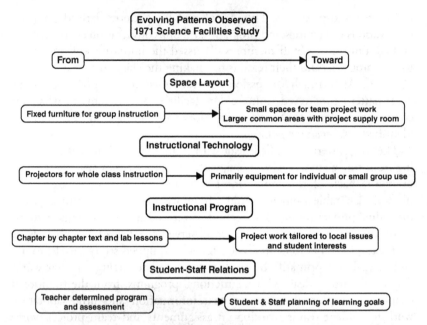

Figure 4.1 Four evolving patterns (shaded cells) observed in our 1971 study of science facilities and programs. These same patterns could be observed in today's schools – with the addition of internet use and current digital technology.

The lesson that we learned is that these evolving patterns, shown in the above figure, are interdependent: one cannot move successfully to a high level on any one of our "evolving patterns" unless the school also moves to higher levels on the other three patterns. This is not easy to accomplish even with the best school leadership, and even then, it takes a sustained effort for a period of years. Later in this chapter and in Chapter 5, I will show examples where real and successful improvements have been accomplished.

The results of our study were published in 1972 by the NSTA as a book (see Figure 4.2). I also authored papers describing the study and results in the Science Teacher and the American Biology Teacher. (See Novak, 1972a; 1972b; 1973.)

Although our study was focused on science facilities and programs, our study team found that in most schools where very traditional science programs and facilities were in use, the same could be said about other instructional programs in the schools. Conversely, the schools that were most "advanced" in their patterns for science were also doing more exemplary work in other subject matter areas. When you consider the fact

Figure 4.2   The NSTA report on our 1971 study of science facilities and programs. The book cover shows a scene at one of the best schools we studied.

that we studied 160 of the most innovative schools out of some 600 nominated across the United States, and that only a dozen or so of those were truly doing innovative work, you have to come away with the picture that educational innovation that is truly innovative and exemplary is relatively rare. I have not found a recent report on school facilities and programs, but I would be surprised to learn that more than a small minority of schools in the United States currently operate truly exemplary school facilities and programs. Later in this chapter and in the next chapter, I shall describe some very good things that are now happening in American schools and colleges.

Since we did our study, the world has moved into the digital internet age. The potential for radically improved education is so much greater. I will present later some studies that suggest there is promise for great improvement in public and private schools that give really great hope that the peoples of the world will become better learners and better educated.

In reflecting back on our study of facilities and programs, it is clear that those few schools that were truly exceptional were doing many of the things that Lev Vygotsky had suggested schools should be doing in his writing in the 1920s and 1930s. He recommended that schools emphasized students working in study teams and taking an active role in planning their learning activities. Unfortunately, Vygotsky's works were published in Russian and relatively few western scholars read Russian. English translations of his works were published in the 1960s and 1980s (Vygotsky, 1962; 1986). We began applying some of his ideas in our research and instructional programs in the late 1960s. For example, Vygotsky put forward the idea of *scaffolding* wherein carefully selected objects or activities could help to model the idea being presented. We made extensive use of this principle in the design of our A-T lessons. We also see the use of simple concept maps as a powerful scaffolding tool.

Although I never heard mention of Vygotsky's work in my school visits, some of the best teachers I met did talk about the importance of students learning from each other. No teacher ever mentioned the importance of recognizing that children learn best when instruction is targeted at the group's general *Zone of Proximal Development*. But I did hear them say how well students can work together to solve real problems and understand what they are doing. This kind of teaching and learning that we saw in the best schools in 1971 is what is now being promulgated under the label of *active learning*. I shall discuss active learning later in this chapter and in Chapter 5.

Learning from a Project with Lompoc, California Public Schools

In the fall of 1988, I received a call from Henry Galena, Assistant Superintendent for Instruction for Lompoc, California Schools. He had read my book, *Learning How to Learn*, and he wanted to implement the ideas presented in the book for all students in Lompoc.

In my first phone conversation with Mr. Galena, I indicated that such an enterprise would take a period of years. He replied he was prepared to stay with the effort for however long it would take for implementation in all Lompoc schools. We agreed to start with elementary school teachers and principals, and I traveled to Lompoc to begin the project. It takes most of a day to get to and from Lompoc from Ithaca, so I did not want to engage in this project if there was not a long-term commitment. Too often in the past, I had met with school administrators eager to adopt some of our work, but after one or two meetings, the project was dropped, usually due to lack of funding.

We had an initial meeting with about twenty elementary school teachers and two principals in the fall of 1988. They were introduced to ideas of meaningful learning, concept mapping and the Vee heuristic. By the end of a two-day session, all of the teachers succeeded in making at least one good concept map for the subject matter they were teaching. The teachers recognized that what we were proposing to do was "revolutionary," and they expressed their enthusiasm for the work. I continued to return to Lompoc, meeting with groups of teachers and their principals about three times per year. There was high enthusiasm among elementary school teachers and principals who were working with the learning strategies and learning tools. I helped them find ways to incorporate the tools and ideas into their instruction. We began to talk about expanding to the junior high schools in the coming school year.

Promising as the innovation program with Lompoc schools appeared to be in 1991, we were again struck down by an unexpected external event. The decision had been made by the US Air Force to drastically reduce the personnel at the Vandenberg Air Force Base near Lompoc, California. This meant the hundreds of children of Vandenberg parents would no longer be attending Lompoc schools. Federal "Impact Funds" paid to Lompoc schools were cut drastically as a result. Funding for our project was eliminated and the Assistant Superintendent I was working with left the system. Thus, ended another project that for a couple of years looked as though it could become a national model.

Unlike almost every other country, public schools in the USA are not controlled by the national government or even by the states. Though both play a role in funding education, the primary funding comes from taxes levied by local school districts. Also, major decisions regarding what is taught and how it is taught are determined by the school boards of over

13,000 school districts in the USA. And of course, local politics play a key role in decisions made in each of these districts. So, if you are wondering why the good things we have learned in the last thirty years to improve teaching and learning are not being widely implemented in our schools, there are no simple answers. But little by little, evidenced-based innovations are occurring in education and I am confident that the future looks bright for substantive improvement in helping people learn in every phase of our lives, from infancy to senescence.

A Success Story in San Jose, Costa Rica

In 2002, Alberto Cañas and I were invited to lecture to faculty and students at the University of Costa Rica. We presented some of the work we had done to improve CmapTools software and some of the research that showed the effectiveness of these tools for facilitating learning. We also discussed the importance of having students work in small groups on problems of their own choosing. In this work, teachers serve as counselors and guides, not the dispensers of information. In short, we were encouraging active learning for students, not a role of passive recipients of information.

One of the persons in our audience, Otto Silesky, was the principal of a special school in San Jose that had been established to work with high school students who were not doing well in traditional classes. Silesky was trained as a psychologist and had extensive experience working with high school children. He found the arguments and data Alberto and I presented very persuasive and he decided he wanted to apply them in his school, the Instituto Educación Integral.

Some of the teachers in Silesky's school were at first reluctant to use concept mapping and to move to small group learning activities. He patiently counseled with these teachers, and in the end all agreed to cooperate and use the new program.

As the school year progressed, both students and teachers became enthusiastic about the new teaching and learning approach. It was therefore somewhat disappointing to everyone when the 2003 State exam results for seniors came in with a lower approval rate of 55 percent. However, both the students and the teachers agreed that the new methods of learning were worth continuing. All agreed that it took time to adapt to a new method of instruction and to become proficient in using CmapTools.

The good news is that in succeeding years, the percent of seniors making "Approval" ratings rose to 92% in 2004, 94%, in 2005, 97% in 2006,

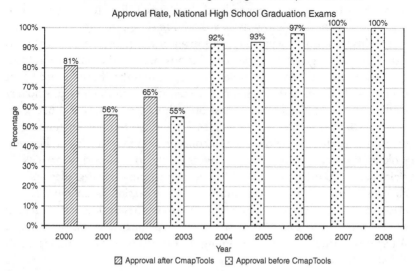

Figure 4.3   Performance of high school seniors at Instituto Educación Integral before and after using concept maps and small group instruction (from Silesky, 2008). If you read Spanish, you can learn more about Silesky's school at: Instituto de Educacion Integral Otto Silesky.

100% in 2007, and 100% again in 2008, the last date for which data was available in Silesky's report (see Figure 4.3). No other high school in Costa Rica matched this achievement.

Actually, the data show that when a school makes a major change in instructional approaches and assessment, it takes years, not months, for teachers and students to be competent with the new approach – if it is a truly significant positive alternative approach (see Karpicke and Blunt, 2011).

In most research studies on the effectiveness of alternative instructional or learning strategies, the duration of the new approach is usually several weeks at best. One absurd study was published in the world-renowned journal, *Science*, by the American Association for the Advancement of Science (see Novak and Cañas, 2004). This study took place with volunteer college psychology students during a one-hour period including a brief 25-minute training session on concept mapping.

Needless to say, the students doing the concept mapping did not do as well on retrieval of information tests at the end of the one-hour session, nor one week later, when compared with students who repeated during the hour memorized text information and a test on this information. Even more absurd, the authors generalized their conclusions to all ages and all disciplines in an interview with *New York Times* reporters (Belluck, 2011).

The first two things a person learns in an introductory statistics course is that you cannot generalize your conclusions beyond the population from which you drew a random sample. The only thing that Karpike and Blunt could validly claim is that a sample of volunteer introductory psychology students who practiced taking a test on a short text passage did better on that test than students in a sample that spent 25 minutes in training to concept map that text and prepare a concept map for that text. When you look at the data in Silesky's multiyear study, the absurdity of making claims about the lack of value of concept mapping in all grades and for all subject matter from a 25-minute training session is obvious. It is a classic example of a psychologist trying to do studies dealing with teaching and learning from the theoretical perspectives of behavioral psychology. A paper pointing out the shortcomings of this study was later published in *Science* (see Cañas et al., 2001).

Learning from a Project in Panamanian Public Schools

The most ambitious project I have been involved with to improve public education took place in Panama during the years 2004 through 2009. Martin Torrĵios was elected president of Panama in September 2004. In addition to the usual goals of advancing economy of the country, President Torrĵios and his colleagues were also committed to beginning a major improvement of public education.

An advisory board was appointed that included leaders in education, industry, and government. The board was charged with the challenge of developing an educational program that would serve as a model to help to leap-frog Panama into a leadership in education in the twenty-first century. Gaspar Tarté, who was Secretary in the Torrĵios cabinet, was chosen to lead the effort. The advisory board sought out innovative programs and leadership that might be considered for the new educational effort in Panama.

The advisory board soon became aware of the outstanding innovative efforts in Latin American education that incorporated some of the work of Alberto Cañas and his colleagues at the IHMC, including the development of the CmapTools software program. Alberto Cañas and his wife Carmen agreed to play a major role in planning and executing the project in Panama.

The advisory board recognized that even with substantial financial resources the transformation of education in Panama's public schools would have to be a stepwise process. Competency training staff were not easy to find, and one was bound to learn a great deal from earlier successes and failures. For various reasons, it was decided to begin the program with students in grades 4, 5, and 6 in 1,000 schools distributed over the ten provinces of Panama. There was evidence that this age group could benefit from computer-assisted instruction and small group work, and then they could become a leadership group as they advanced through school. The plan was to bring the principles and all of the teachers for participating schools to Panama City for a two-week training program. Since more than half of the teachers had never used a computer, this proved to be a challenge at the beginning, but as the training strategies improved, all teachers were successful in acquiring the necessary skills. Thus, Project Conéctaté al Conocimiento, as it was called, got underway in Panama in late 2004.

During the years 2004–2009, the project was funded by the Panamanian government and had strong support from President Torrĵios and all members of his cabinet, especially Gaspar Tarté, Secretary for Education and director of the project. The goals included providing special training for all teachers and principals in grades 4, 5, and 6 in 1,000 schools. Their training consisted of instruction in meaningful learning strategies, including concept mapping and the use of computers and the Internet. President Torrĵios and Gaspar Tarté took a keen interest in the project and visited participating schools a number of times. On one occasion Joan and I visited his school with the President and the Secretary. We were impressed with how engaged they became with the work the students were doing.

Joan and I visited Panama on three different occasions. On one of these visits, we were invited to meet with President Torrĵios in his office to discuss some of the theoretical foundations that were developed in our research program and were the foundation for this project. As a graduate in agricultural science from North Carolina State University, not only was the President fluent in English, but he asked very good questions about my theoretical ideas. Alberto Cañas and his wife and a few other project leaders were also present at this meeting in the President's office.

There were many challenges initially, since equipment needed to be purchased and installed in schools. In extreme situations, solar power facilities were needed for computers and satellite internet connections where there were no existing power lines. Alberto Cañas and his wife Carmen played a major role in training the leadership for the project, as well as conducting numerous workshops with teachers and principals. The staff devised many interesting training tools, including the use of large wooden dies with words on the six faces. Participants could look for ways to build a concept map using the words that came up as two dies were tossed. The game illustrated the many ways in which concepts can be combined into meaningful propositions.

On our second visit to Panama, Joan and I had plane problems and feared we could not make the trip. Fortunately, President Torrĵios was a friend of the president of Copa Airlines. After a few phone calls, they made room for us on a flight from Miami to Panama City. We were met at the airport by several cabinet members and ushered into a private room where we were served tea and snacks while aids took care of getting our passports stamped and our baggage loaded into a limousine. The next day we met with President Torrĵios in his office, and a few other people as noted earlier.

While the implementation varied in quality from school to school, by the end of the five-year effort most of the teachers in grades 4 to 6 in the 1,000 participating schools were successful in using CmapTools and other strategies to improve teaching and learning. Students were encouraged to make some of their own resources. This may have been as simple as taking photos or videos of pertinent events and objects or the creation of a play or exposition that illustrated all they were learning. Some of the team reports were in the form of a large concept map.

From the beginning, the project was designed to include schools in every province of Panama. This proved to be challenging in terms of both getting project staff and teachers back and forth from Panama City and providing reliable electric power and internet service to schools.

In many of the rural locations, Project Conéctaté was especially helpful in that it provided internet access to family and friends anywhere in the world during evening hours and on weekends. This contributed to the adult support of the project.

Some remarkably good class projects were completed, such as that illustrated in Figure 4.4. Even in rural areas, teachers and students were successful in using computers and the Internet for learning. Parents in many communities used the facilities in the evening to contact family in other cities and countries.

Figure 4.4 shows one of the team project reports that was prepared in the form of a concept map. Icons on the bottom of large concept ovals opened other digital resources, such as photos and videos, many of which the students had prepared. This report on their study of Kuna Indians portrayed life on the islands near Panama where the Kuna Indians still live today, and which is a popular tourist attraction.

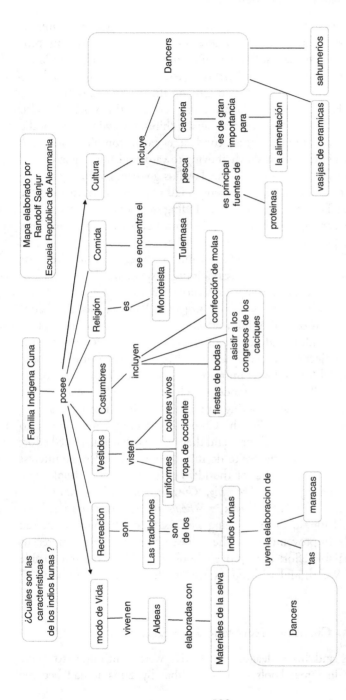

Figure 4.4 A "Familia Indigence" concept map prepared by one of the student teams involved in this project. Many of the resources shown in the concept map were also prepared by team members.

Joan and I visited Panama three times. I gave lectures to teams of teachers and principals, as well as to government officials, university professors, and project managers. We were hosted most graciously, including a personal meeting with President Torrĵios noted earlier. Joan recalls talking with one of the students who was working on the Internet and building a concept map. He commented: "I really like learning this way!" We also enjoyed a private tour of the Panama Canal Exhibit, reviewing some of the history of the canal and plans for a second larger canal, completed in 2016.

The Conéctaté project was slowly moving toward realizing its goals when national elections led to the loss of the Torrĵios government in 2009. The new government, in typical Latin American fashion, tossed out most of the programs of the Torrĵios government, including the Conéctaté project. We do not know what happened to the equipment, but without governmental support of the program, we surmise that all of the accomplishments and hard work of Carmen and Alberto Cañas and the other team members was soon lost. This was one more disappointing experience I have had in working to improve education in a substantial way.

Disappointing as the collapse of the project in Panama was, the record shows that this kind of radical improvement in school education, exploiting the use of new ideas and new technology, is possible on a nationwide scale. Had the project continued for another five or ten years, it might have become the model for dramatic improvement of education in developing countries. It is possible that the model may be picked up by Costa Rica or Colombia, where many are working to implement similar programs.

There is also the chance that the Chinese government may choose to support a similar project in China – and they can marshal a sustained effort to accomplish this if they choose to do this. There is considerable interest for China to implement some of the ideas presented in this book. The second edition of my book *Learning, Creating, and Using Knowledge: Concept Maps and Facilitative Tools in Schools and Corporations* has been translated into Chinese and it is being well received. We have witnessed the remarkable improvements in the infrastructure in China in recent years. A comparable effort to improve schooling could lead to remarkable achievements. We should all keep an eye on changes that may occur in education in China.

Creating a New Model for Education

Alberto Cañas and his colleagues at IHMC were continuing to make improvements in CmapTools software so that by 2003 it had become very easy to attach digital materials to concepts or linking words. These materials became part of the digital file for the concept maps. We had been using this feature of CmapTools more frequently in various projects conducted by me and by Alberto. Moreover, the amount of material available on the Internet had continued to grow exponentially. It had reached a point where any person could access digital information on any topic, and most of this was available at no cost to the user. It occurred to me that we had reached a point where we could use CmapTools to build what we were calling a New Model for Education (Novak, 2004; Novak and Cañas, 2004).

The key idea in the New Model was to use as a starting point for any learning experience a small "expert skeleton" concept map as a beginning for the exploration of a specific domain of knowledge. The idea is that a small concept map (six to twelve concepts) would be prepared by an expert on the subject to be studied, and this would be used as a starting point for a small group of students who would then use all the many resources available to them to build on this "expert skeleton" map and work to elaborate it, drawing on the full range of resources available to the group and especially internet resources.

The "expert skeleton" map serves to "scaffold" the group's learning and then provides the foundation for building a much more elaborate "knowledge model" or "knowledge portfolio." Over a span of days or even weeks, the study groups would engage in many of these activities available to any group to learn, as shown in Figure 4.5.

As members of the group engage in a variety of learning activities suggested in the small ovals in Figure 4.5, they would build on the concept map and add links to a variety of digital resources they found or created to build a more comprehensive knowledge model. This model is illustrated in Figure 4.6.

It is to be expected that as the group begins to gather information on the focus question of their "expert skeleton" concept map, some groups, or maybe most of them, will decide that there is a better "expert skeleton" concept map for their inquiry. When a group of students work together using the learning tools and ideas we are suggesting, it is remarkable how thoughtful and productive these groups can be.

As groups of learners create knowledge models, these can be easily stored in digital files and become a record of the learners' achievement. They can also be used as new starting points for future, more advance study, or for other study groups interested in this subject matter. The posters and other exhibits created by study groups can be excellent materials to post in the

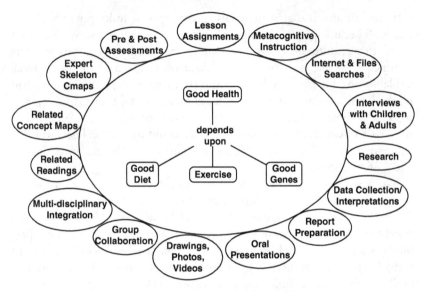

Figure 4.5   A beginning map structure for building a concept map for "Good Health."

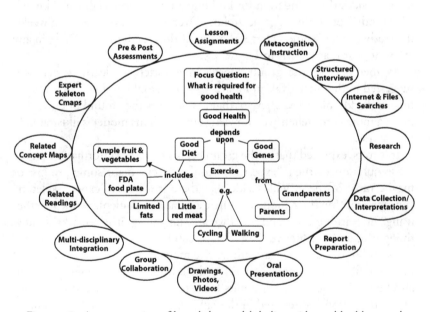

Figure 4.6   A representation of knowledge model dealing with good health created by a working group.

hallway on tack boards or walls to illustrate the achievement of these groups to parents or other groups. We shall see some examples of this in Chapter 5.

Our New Model for Education does not ignore the important role that teachers and curriculum planners can play in establishing educational goals for schools. They can contribute by developing sets of "expert skeleton concept maps" to be used as starting points for learning at any grade level and for any school subject. Moreover, the New Model easily accommodates the desirable practice of having mixed age groups working together on projects. Older students may bring some knowledge and skills helpful to younger students. On the other hand, the kinds of questions younger students ask about any topic may stimulate more creative thinking by older students. We will return to this discussion in Chapter 5 of this book.

A Look to the Future

Looking Back to See Forward

Here are a few quotes from famous people:[1]

> We spend a great deal of time studying history, which, let's face it, is mostly the history of stupidity. —Stephen Hawking

> That men do not learn very much from the lessons of history is the most important of all the lessons of history. —Aldous Huxley

> If men could learn from history, what lessons it might teach us! But passion and party blind our eyes, and the light which experience gives us is a lantern on the stern which shines only on the waves behind. —Samuel Taylor Coleridge

I was eleven years old when World War II began for the USA on December 7, 1941, when the Japanese bombed Pearl Harbor. The war began in Europe in 1939 with the German invasion of Poland, and the Italian invasion of Albania and Greece. In 1937, Japan had invaded China. Clearly the world had not learned the lesson from World War I: If good people do not band together to prevent despots from taking over the reins of government, bad things will happen. But sometimes it is not easy to define who are the bad guys and who are the good guys. We faced this problem in Korea in the early 1950s and in Vietnam in the 1960s, and in the Middle East today. The problems are not new; they go back at least to Greek and Roman times.

As a young child, it seemed to me that wars are in general a terrible thing, and intelligent, good, and rational people should be able to find ways to prevent wars and advance peace and harmony. As my studies progressed and I learned more about things we are doing wrong in

---

[1] "The Lessons of History Famous Quotations and Quotes," *age-of-the-sage.org*. www.age-of-the sage .org/history/quotations/lessons of history.html

educating people and things that show more promise, I sought to pursue a career that would help people become better learners and better thinkers and committed to helping make this a better world for everyone. This book is probably my last major effort to help the world achieve this goal.

In earlier chapters I have tried to present what I think we have learned to help people learn and also to become better at creating new knowledge and more committed to making this a better world for everyone. In this chapter, I will present what I think are some promising ideas and trends that might be pursued more vigorously. It is my hope that at least some small percentage of readers of this book will choose to share my goals.

My dad set an example for me. He was always reading, usually in bed after a long busy day. He read the *Minneapolis Star* and also subscribed to *Karpatska Rus*, a weekly paper published in Carpathian Russian, the language he spoke in his home village of Dubova, Austro-Hungary, which is now Slovakia. I was born in 1930, at the height of the Great Depression, and the family was always short of money. My dad became active in politics, and I often helped to distribute political papers in our neighborhood prior to elections. I recall working on the campaign to elect Hubert Humphrey Mayor of Minneapolis in 1945, and later, in 1948, on his election to the Senate. Dad taught me that good things don't just happen; it takes hard work on the part of good people. His teachings motivated and sustained me in the most difficult professional challenges I have had in my career. As noted in Chapter 1, Dad's teachings were a huge influence on me in my career. For a man whose formal education ended in grade 4 in Dubova, Dad was in his own way quite the scholar.

My early experiences with politics and campaigning as a child led me to a lifelong interest in politics. I watched as Humphrey moved from Mayor of Minneapolis to Minnesota Senator in 1948 and Vice President with President Johnson in 1965 to 1969. Johnson had inherited the Vietnam War and he sought to end it by escalating US troop involvement throughout his administration. The war became increasingly unpopular with young people, with numerous protests against the war taking place all over the United States. It was also a time when there were numerous protests for Black rights and equality for woman's rights. Since the Democratic Party and President Johnson were in control of the White House, the protest movements probably contributed to Humphrey's loss in a presidential campaign against Richard Nixon in 1968. Nixon campaigned on the promise that he had a secret plan to defeat the North Vietnamese quickly, but no such plan ever materialized. In the end, a withdrawal plan was negotiated in 1975. Recently it was reported by John A. Farrell (*New York*

Times, Dec. 31, 2016) that President Johnson had sought to negotiate a settlement in 1968 when H. R. Haldeman, Nixon's closest aide, revealed that Nixon in fact directed his campaign's efforts to scuttle peace talks over fears it might grant his opponent, Vice President Hubert H. Humphrey, an edge in the 1968 election.[2] How many American troops and Vietnamese lost their lives because of this we will never know.

Today we have relatively good relations with Vietnam, and it is a popular tourist destination and active trading partner. Well, live and learn – maybe?

I thought the tragedy of the Vietnam War and the failure to see the resulting horrors of communism that reportedly would follow a North Vietnam victory might convince the peoples of the world that war is not a solution to our problems. This did not occur. Instead with United States Republican leadership, we launched another foolish war in Iraq in March 2003. President Bush claimed "Mission Accomplished" in May 2003 in front of a banner on a ship, but we all know now that this was not true. When will our presidents speak the truth to the American people?

History repeated itself when Donald Trump campaigned in 2016 saying that he knew better than the generals how to bring peace quickly to the Middle East. No such peace is in sight as this is written.

Lessons from the History of Education

When, in 1952, as a graduate student I began to be serious about the study of education, I enrolled in a course, The History of Education. The course began with a discussion of the great Greek scholar Socrates who taught in the fifth century BC. Socrates developed a strategy of asking a series of questions, and through his questioning, he could lead his pupils to understand the ideas he wished to convey. I was struck by the power of this Socratic method when I observed it in practice by my best Botany Department professor, Ernst Abbe, who would pick up a plant from the greenhouse and bring it to class. He would then proceed to ask questions about the plant, gradually leading us to understand something special about the plant, and perhaps then moving on to have us study the plant further by preparing microscope slides of sections of the plant. I loved the way Abbe taught us to form our own questions, and over time to formulate

---

[2] "This Day in History: Last US Combat Troops Withdraw from Vietnam," *VOA News*, March 29, 2017. www.voanews.com/a/last-united-states-combat-troops-withdraw-from-vietnam-this-day-in-1973/3786745.html.

our own answers to plant structures and their functions. Using the Socratic method of teaching is not easy and many, if not most teachers, never master this technique.

Throughout my five years of graduate studies in the Botany Department at Minnesota, Professor Abbe often chided me for studying education. He often said that there has been nothing new in education since the time of Socrates. Rather than discouraging me, I took this as a challenge because I believed that there must be ways to approach education more as a science if we could develop principles and perhaps a theory to guide the improvement of education. Gradually I was forming the goal of proving Professor Abbe wrong by finding ways to develop principles and a theory of education; however, improvement of educational practice is never easy. I also saw the need for developing new ways to make records of learning, and study education, and also new educational tools. Little did I know how the coming world transformation would affect education.

The History of Education course moved on to famous Renaissance educators such as Rousseau, Pestalozzi, and his protégé, Froebel. The common theme in all of these famous historical people in education was that they saw the principal job of the teacher as patiently guiding the learner toward understanding whatever the lesson dealt with. By contrast, most of the schools at that time saw the student's role as memorizing information verbatim from texts or teachers' lectures and reciting this back to the class or answering simplistic questions. This was later followed by students answering true–false and multiple-choice questions the teacher or book author prepared. This was the principal educational strategy employed when I went to school in the 1930s and 1940s. Unfortunately, far too many teachers today do what these famous educators condemned, except that they now can use machine-scored true–false and multiple-choice tests to quickly assess student's learning.

It should be noted that the root of the word "educate" is the Latin word *ēdūcō*, meaning to lead or to lead forth. In many ways, my career as an educator has been an effort to find better ways of leading learners to build their own understandings. I think the History of Education course I took many years ago, combined with some very good Socratic teaching from a few of my best teachers, profoundly shaped my ideas on what should be the goals for good education.

The History of Education course ended with a discussion of John Dewey and his efforts to create a Laboratory School at the University of Chicago in 1896. Dewey attempted to use ideas from the developing field of psychology together with ideas from some of the famous educators

Figure 5.1   Photo of one of John Dewey's lab school classrooms. Note that children are working in small groups on tables on various learning activities. There are not the usual rows of single child desks (Yahoo search).

mentioned earlier. He encouraged his teachers to work with small groups of students, and to guide them in their inquiry into whatever the subject matter was for this age group.

Dewy believed that children should work in small groups on real problems, rather than routine textbook lessons (see Figure 5.1). For example, to learn about ratio and proportions in math, he suggested children work out solutions for making smaller or larger portions for any recipe. To learn about plant life cycles, he thought children could work in small groups to plant different seeds in a school garden or on window shelves and observe the plants growing from germinating seeds to mature plants producing flowers and then a new crop of seeds. Throughout these activities, students should be encouraged to discuss with their peers what they think is happening and why. In short, he thought active learning should be the dominant activity in school learning. This idea is now becoming common in pedagogical literature, but the idea is not new. I will discuss this idea more extensively later in this chapter.

Dewey and his wife had trouble recruiting the kind of teachers they wanted. After all, most of the teachers were trained in college classes where the predominant activities they did were to memorize information in texts or lectures with the goal of answering questions dealing primarily with trivial details they had memorized. Dewey and his wife worked diligently to recruit and train teachers who could lead active learning groups. Despite their best efforts, the school floundered after Dewey left, and the school was closed in 1904.

Dewey is also well known for his philosophical writings. He believed that knowledge comes from human problem-solving. Since problems change over time, he regarded knowledge as constantly changing. In many ways, he was one of the first philosophers to see knowledge as constantly changing and evolving. He was perhaps the first philosopher to subscribe to what we now call *constructivist* epistemology, rather than the positivist and later logical positivist philosophy discussed earlier in this book.

Many universities have created "laboratory schools" with the goal of doing and applying good educational research to the improvement of teaching and learning. I did my intern teaching at such a school at the University of Minnesota in 1951–1952. I never saw any evidence that any of the teaching done there was based on research and incorporated the best ideas that came from research findings in education or psychology. Indeed, the teaching I saw there was primarily marching students through a textbook chapter by chapter with weekly quizzes on information memorized and monthly or semester tests that were more of the same. Nevertheless, Minnesota was regarded nationally as one of the best schools of education!

I recall my efforts as a teaching intern in 1951–1952 trying instructional approaches that would help my students understand the key ideas in the material we were studying. None of the supervising teachers I had that year supported these efforts, and I received B grades in all three-quarters of my intern teaching. It was my impression that what my supervising teachers wanted me to do was nothing like what I observed my best Botany Department professors doing. Reflecting on that experience years later, when I was engaged in science teacher training at Purdue University and later at Cornell University, it helped me to understand why so much school science teaching fails to help students understand the science they are studying – and to value and appreciate the conceptual grandeur that scientists have achieved.

Seeking Ways to Enhance Social Responsibility

One of the lessons I learned from my dad was that while it is important to strive to do the best we can to take care of our family, and ourselves,

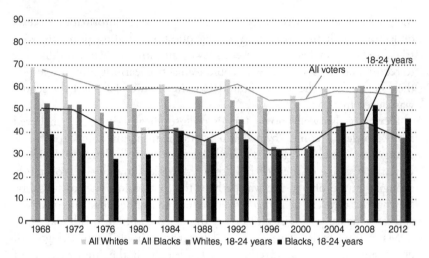

Figure 5.2   US Census Bureau data on voting percentages over the years:
race and age group.

we should also seek to try to make the world a better place for
everyone. Just how one could help improve the lives of people will
vary from person to person. However, probably most would agree that
such commitment requires as a minimum taking responsibility to vote
in local, state, and national elections. The percent of eligible voters who
actually vote varies year to year but seldom exceeds 60% in national
elections and 25% in local elections (US Census Dept.). As Figure 5.2
shows, less than 60% of eligible voters vote, and only about 45% of
18 to 24-year-olds vote in national elections. Obviously, there is a huge
number of potential voters who do not take voting seriously. In
Sweden, by comparison, the average voter turnout rate has been about
85% for the last forty years.

A Study with College Chemistry Students

Stacey Lowery Bretz, one my best Ph.D. students, was interested in
finding better ways to interest students studying college chemistry to
seek a deeper understanding of chemistry. She was also interested in
assessing students' views on the value of chemistry for understanding
socially important issues. She chose to work with students taking a
general education chemistry course taught by Professor Meinwald at
Cornell University.

The typical introductory general education courses in most sciences present only a superficial coverage of information from that science. What they fail to do is to provide instruction on how scientists in any field build on important principles and established research strategies to gain new insights and ideas. Bretz and Meinwald (2001) developed a course that engaged small groups of students working together on real problem-solving on topics currently being researched by chemists.

Meinwald and his research group had spent twenty years studying the chemistry of pheromones. Pheromones are chemical compounds produced by insects and other organisms that serve to attract other insects for mating or other events favorable to them, or to ward off possible enemies. Meinwald and his colleagues had numerous examples from their research work with pheromones, and these served as one of the problem areas provided to the introductory chemistry course students. Students learned how to use the processes and tools chemists employ to discover the chemistry that underlies various aspects of life, including chromatography, mass spectrometry, ultraviolet spectroscopy, nuclear magnetic resonance (NMR) imaging, and X-ray crystallography. They learned more than the information about the topic of study; they also learned about the methodologies used to acquire new information about the topics of study. The course was designed not only to teach some important principles of chemistry, but also to impact the feelings students had toward science through small group work on real research problems. It was a goal of the course to move students toward deeper understanding of the science of chemistry and also to gain some understanding of how new knowledge is created in the field. Bretz saw this course as a good case study for her Ph.D. thesis research (1994).

In Chapter 3, I discussed the continuing efforts of our research group to develop and refine a theory of education. I discussed the important role that meaningful learning plays in acquiring and understanding new knowledge. I also discussed the important role that feelings play in the acquisition of new knowledge. Based on these ideas, we had developed what we called a Learning Strategies Questionnaire that was discussed in Chapter 3. Bretz saw this as a useful tool for her Ph.D. study using students in Meinwald's Case Studies chemistry course.

The Learning Strategies Questionnaire contained seventeen items, each of which provided choices from strongly disagree to strongly agree. There was also space left between items to write in comments. The first item is shown below. The complete questionnaire is given in Appendix 1.

1. **In general, I put in a lot of effort to try to understand things which initially seem obscure.**
   SD   D   U   A   SA
   Comments:

A majority of the items were written so that a subject responding Strongly Agree (SA) would be scored as inclined toward meaningful learning while those marking the item Strongly Disagree (SD) would be inclined toward rote learning. Six of the items were written to reverse the answers for meaningful learning. A few of the items dealt with the learner's views on the nature of knowledge and new knowledge creation. Bretz used this Questionnaire to identify a sample of students who were highly inclined toward meaningful learning and another sample of students highly inclined toward rote learning. She prepared concept maps from these interviews, two of which are shown in Figures 5.3 and 5.4.

Stacey summarized her research findings in the abstract of her thesis as follows:

1. Rote (learning) males viewed learning and science literacy in terms of the amount of knowledge they had, whereas their female counterparts emphasized the processes of receiving such knowledge. Meaningful male learners spoke not of passive processes, but rather of making connections between knowledge they had and knowledge they wanted to learn. Meaningful learner females focused on making connections between domains of knowledge, e.g., biology and chemistry, with hopes for applying their knowledge and solving problems. Contextual interpretation of these conceptions of learning and science literacy showed that a core curriculum making explicit commitments to shared meanings and incorporating opportunities for meaningful learning provided students a skill broadly transferable to science literacy: e.g., learning how to learn (from Bretz, 1994).

Clearly the course Meinwald and Bretz offered did not achieve 100% success in moving students toward high levels of meaningful learning and much enhanced commitment to become socially responsible citizens. No single course could achieve this. Nevertheless, it was evident that many of their students had enhanced their understanding that chemistry can help to deal with significant societal problems – and they regarded this as important. Bretz and Meinwald continued to work with this course and described the course and student outcomes in a paper published in 2001.

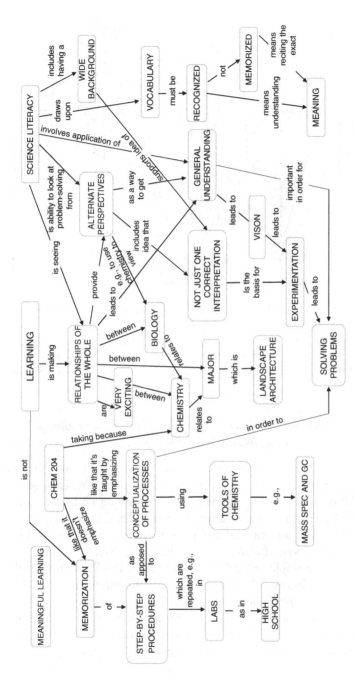

Figure 5.3   A concept map prepared by Bretz from an interview with a student committed to meaningful learning. For this student learning is "very exciting" and involves "making relationships of the whole." This student sees learning vocabulary as necessary for "general understanding" and so it is not just memorizing. The end goal is solving problems (Bretz, 1994).

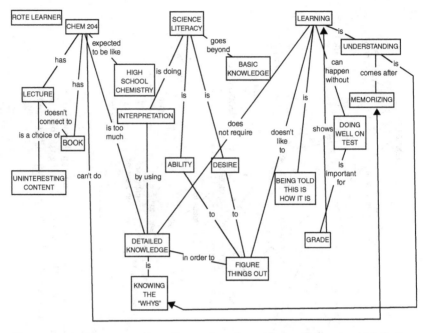

Figure 5.4   A concept map drawn from an interview with a student scoring high for rote learning. For this student memorizing is the key to learning chemistry; understanding comes after memorizing and detailed knowledge is necessary to figure things out.

A Lesson from My Work with the Schreyer Honors College at Pennsylvania State University

During the 1996–1997 academic year, I was invited by Dean Cheryl Achterberg to serve as a senior advisor to the Schreyer Honors College at Penn State University. Cheryl was one of my outstanding Ph.D. students at Cornell University. She was committed to the idea that the improvement of nutrition and nutrition education required improving theoretical foundations (Achterberg, Novak, and Gillespie, 1985). The Honors College was made possible primarily by grants from the William A. and Joan Schreyer Foundation. Schreyer was formerly the chairman and CEO at Merrill Lynch, a prominent American investment company. The Schreyers hoped that the Honors College would select students who not only were outstanding academically but also demonstrated a commitment to try to make contributions to society in general. The general goal was similar to that sought by Carbonero et al. (2017) in a program for secondary school students that I will discuss later. Cheryl Achterberg hoped that I might help develop admission criteria that would better select the kind of socially committed students the Schreyer Foundation wanted to support.

I was also asked to help with faculty development by offering seminars that would encourage faculty not only to become more proficient in teaching their subject matter but also to seek ways to encourage their students to use their knowledge to improve the lives of people. This was also a time when I was working to revise and enhance my theory of education to include more emphasis on the role of feelings in learning and doing educational tasks more effectively. I saw the work with Penn State as an opportunity to explore further some of the ideas I was developing on the relationship between meaningful learning and social commitment. The work of Bretz and Meinwald suggested that the Learning Approach Questionnaire we had used in her study could be a useful tool in a study that would focus on factors that lead to students with greater commitment to social responsibility. I was interested in testing the idea I had been developing that the best way to enhance students' commitment to social responsibility was to help them achieve high levels of meaningful learning. The work with the Schreyer honors students became part of the supporting evidence for the theory of education I presented in Chapter 3.

The questionnaire was mailed to senior students in the Schreyer honors program. After reviewing the results from the questionnaires, we decided to interview individual students to probe more deeply their ideas on their approach to learning and their ideas on the nature of knowledge and new knowledge creation. In general, we found that student responses in our interviews closely paralleled their responses on the questionnaire. During the interviews we also asked the students what they hoped to do in the future. With regard to the questioning on the nature of knowledge and knowledge creation, those inclined toward rote learning usually had little to say or simply said they had no idea how new knowledge was created. In contrast those most inclined toward meaningful learning said that knowledge comes from new research or is produced by creative people. I recall one of the students with the highest meaningful learning score commented that new knowledge comes from people who are obsessive in their search for new answers. The results from this study, even though it was cut short by the end of the school year and my tenure at Penn State, contributed to my thinking regarding my theory of education. The results strongly supported the idea that meaningful learning underlies the constructive integration of thinking, feeling, and acting, leading to empowerment of the individual for commitment and responsibility.

An unanticipated positive result related to this study occurred at the Dean's reception for graduating seniors in the Schreyer Honors College. Mr. and Mrs. Schreyer were in attendance and Mrs. Schreyer went about asking the graduates what they planned to do when they left Penn State. Late in the reception she remarked to Cheryl Achterberg how different the future goals of the students were. She pointed to one young lady who told her that she hoped to find a job that would pay very well and that she could retire early. She pointed to a young man who said he probably would be going on to graduate school, but his real goal was to find a career where he could make a positive difference to society. It turned out that Cheryl remembered the girl was the one who had the highest rote learning score on our learning approach questionnaire and the young man was the one who had the highest meaningful learning score on the questionnaire. Admittedly, two students out of the class of thirty hardly provide proof positive. Nevertheless, the remarkable parallel between what we anticipated for the future of these two students closely matched what they said to Mrs. Schreyer.

The stories presented above are far from the kind of rigorous research that needs to be done to establish that meaningful learning is the necessary foundation for developing young people who accept the responsibility and have the commitment to seek to make a positive difference in the world – whatever field of endeavor they choose to pursue. At this point in my career, I must leave further testing of my theory to younger people in universities and other organizations. As noted earlier, simply stated, my theory of education is this: Meaningful learning underlies the constructive integration of thinking, feeling, and acting leading to empowerment for commitment and responsibility. It has taken decades for scientists to provide proof of Einstein's theory that: Energy equals mass times the square of the velocity of light in centimeters ($E=MC^2$). Now we know why the stars produce so much heat and light for billions of years and why hydrogen bombs can be so destructive. There is nothing this elegant in my theory, but it is at least a starting point for making educating a science.

Some Problems of Instruction and Assessment

Multiple-choice tests have been the dominant form of testing in the United States since the early twentieth century. Frederick Kelly completed his doctoral thesis in 1914 at Kansas State University. He advocated tests using a question followed by five possible answers, only one of which is the correct choice. Tests of this kind could be easily scored and were "objective," since the items are usually constructed so as to have only one correct answer. Unlike written or essay answers, no "subjective" interpretation of the answer is required. There are, of course, subjective judgments made in selection of the information to be tested for, and in the structuring of the questions and alternative answer choices. However, the scoring of the items is totally "objective," and anyone with an answer key can score the exam. With the development of scoring machines and answer sheets designed to be used on these machines, thousands of exams can be "objectively scored" at relatively low cost and very quickly.

Objective testing became popular after the use of these tests by the military in World War I and continued during World War II and beyond. This undoubtedly encouraged the use of such tests by schools, businesses, and other organizations. The widespread use of objective tests led to the formation of corporations devoted to preparing and scoring these tests. The Educational Testing Service (ETS) was formed in 1947 in Princeton, New Jersey and is today the largest organization preparing, scoring, and selling testing services. One of my first former Ph.D. students, William Kastrinos, joined the ETS in 1961 and continued there for the remainder of his career. ETS pays its employees and board members relatively high salaries. Needless to say, ETS and similar organizations are a strong political force on issues dealing with educational testing. ETS operates as a private not-for-profit organization and its financial dealings are not publicized. However, some reports indicate their total sales are in excess of 1 billion dollars annually.

When I designed my Ph.D. thesis research in 1956, I became interested in issues of test validity and reliability. Reliability is the ability to provide the same tests score for individuals with the same knowledge or ability. Validity is the extent to which a test accurately measures the true abilities we wish to assess. Multiple-choice tests that have relatively high reliability are fairly easy to design, especially when most of the test items require no more than verbatim recall of information. However, if we seek also to assess the extent to which a learner understands and can reason with information learned, we may have a test with higher validity, but relatively low reliability. This results because so many students who score high on recall of information they have memorized often score low on test items that require reasoning or making valid inferences based on information they memorized. The net effect of including a significant number of tests items that require a higher level of reasoning is that these items tend to lower the scores of most of the students and lead to lower test reliability statistics – something test makers decry. I refer to this problem as "the psychometric trap." Professional test writers usually deal with this problem by deleting these "reasoning" items from the final test. I have discussed this problem more fully in other works (Novak, 1961; 2010).

There have been hundreds of research studies which show that students who memorize information about some phenomenon may still retain misconceptions about that phenomenon. For example, there is a widely shown video made by Harvard Private Universe Project that shows 21 out of 23 Harvard graduates, alumni, and faculty could not give a satisfactory explanation for why we have seasons, a topic that most have studied several times in their schooling. The most common misconception is that the Earth is warmer when it is closer to the sun and colder when it is further away (Schneps and Sadler, 1989). They may remember that the Earth's orbit is somewhat elliptical and give this for a reason for warmer weather in summers. Actually, the Earth is a little closer to the sun during Boston winters, and of course their explanation ignores the fact that the southern hemisphere is colder when the northern hemisphere is warmer. The actual reason for seasonal differences in temperature is due to the tilt of the Earth on its axis, with the North Pole pointing more directly toward the sun during Boston summer, and more away from the sun in winter. The same is true for places in the southern hemisphere, except that higher and lower temperatures come six months later, or earlier, depending on when you start observing.

Misconceptions, once anchored in cognitive structure, are notoriously difficult to displace. They become embedded in a complex of concepts and propositions that are not easily modified. Moreover, there are often strong affective linkages that may influence receptivity to new relevant concepts and propositions needed to remediate the misconception. Only a sustained program of high-quality meaningful learning stands much of a chance to remediate such misconceptions (Novak, 2003). I presented an example of this in Chapter 3 dealing with the Earth in space and the nature of gravity. This problem exists in every subject matter area, but especially in politics.

There have been hundreds of studies that show the persistence of misconceptions even after what appeared to be successful instruction. We held five international conferences on research dealing with misconceptions in science and mathematics. The first was held at Cornell University in 1983 (see Helm and Novak, 1983) and the last one was held in 1995. One of my former Ph.D. students, Robert Abrams, assisted in planning some of these seminars on misconceptions and he maintains a website (www.mlrg.org) where all of the *Proceedings* can be downloaded at no charge.

For almost 100 years, there have been scholars and universities doing research on the successes and failures in science and mathematics education. This kind of research increased greatly after the NSF began funding education research studies in the 1950s, and it significantly accelerated funding for the past thirty years. Much of this research pointed out that our schools were far from achieving desirable levels of student understanding of key ideas of science and mathematics. Some studies showed that most students had little understanding of the methods by which science and mathematics is advanced. Some of this research pointed out that schools teach what was needed to pass standardized achievement tests and these were woefully inadequate in assessing the depth of students' understanding of major concepts and principles. Compared with students in most developed countries, US students were near the bottom on these tests.

Creation of the National Assessment of Educational Progress (NAEP)

In 1988, Congress created the National Assessment Governing Board to set policy for the National Assessment of Educational Progress (NAEP). It is administered by the National Center for Education Statistics (NCES), within the Institute of Education Sciences (IES), a division of the US Department of Education. As the ongoing national indicator of the academic achievement of US students, NAEP regularly collects information on representative samples of students in grades 4, 8, and 12 and periodically reports on student achievement in reading, mathematics, writing, science, and other subject areas. NAEP scores are always reported at the aggregate level, not for individual students or schools. (By law, NAEP cannot report results for individual students.) For science, NAEP results are reported at the national and state levels and for a number of large urban districts. The district reports are provided for urban school systems that volunteer for the Trial Urban District Assessment component of NAEP.

Given the many layers of bureaucracy that are involved in the preparation of the NAEP tests, it is not surprising to learn that any attempt to significantly modify the nature of the exams would be effectively impossible. My good friend Richard Shavelson, former dean of the Graduate

School of Education at Stanford University, sat on the committee to prepare new guidelines for the 2015 NAEP exams in science and mathematics. He and a few other colleagues tried valiantly to include concept mapping and other assessment forms in the 2015 exams. Their efforts were essentially brushed aside by the governing board for NAEP. My only hope is that as schools continue to move in the direction of more student activity-based teaching and learning, the whole NAEP program will collapse from its own dead weight. Some of the changes now being forced upon schools by the widespread problems caused by the Covid-19 pandemic may contribute to this collapse.

There are also international testing programs in science and mathematics, many of which have voluntary participation. While it is difficult to judge the quality of science and mathematics education programs in those schools that choose to participate in international testing, one can be fairly certain that they are not among the lowest performing school districts. Nevertheless, students in American schools consistently rank relatively low on these tests, ranking 20th to 30th when compared with other nations participating in these assessments.

The No Child Left Behind Program in the USA

The comparatively unfavorable performance on science and mathematics tests by American students when matched with students in other developed countries was one of the factors that led Congress to establish the NAEP in 1988. The rationale behind the program was that if schools were engaged in large-scale testing of students in several grades and in several subject areas, these data would lead to improvements in areas of weakness identified. There was also some supplemental funding of programs, but relatively little change in the teaching and learning activities in American classrooms. American students continued to underperform when compared with students in other advanced democracies.

The US Congress again acted to establish a new program to improve education in American schools. In 2001, Congress passed the No Child Left Behind (NCLB) Act. The program was implemented in 2002 and required states to test all students in grades 3–8 and once in high school for competence in English and mathematics. The goal was that by setting high standards and testing for student achievement of these standards, public school education could be improved. Diane Ravitch, Assistant Secretary for Education, was a strong advocate for the program. What Ravitch and many other supporters had not anticipated is that the limitations of multiple-choice testing would lead most schools to do little more than prepare students to memorize answers for typical NCLB test questions. Four years after lavishing praise on the program, Ravitch published *The Death and Life of the Great American School System*. In this book she points out that what occurred is that schools found ways to game the system to improve test scores, but real teaching and learning declined. Some of the decline was due to what Hoffmann (1962) described in his book, *The Tyranny of Testing*. By 2015, the NCLB program was quietly dropped. We shall see later in this book that some more promising alternatives are emerging.

Once again, the primary criteria for school performance were the typical standardized objective tests, administered under national guidelines. The program also included penalties in the form of reduced funding for those schools that repeatedly underperformed on these standardized tests. Moreover, many school districts moved to adjust teacher salaries based on the level of performance of their students. This made the testing program for the NCLB program very "high stakes" testing in many school districts. A high percentage of teachers soon found it was to their best interest to drill students on questions from previous exams and to focus most classroom instruction on activities that would lead to high test scores.

The unintended consequences of the poorly conceived NCLB program have been that in the majority of school districts where this program has been implemented, the quality of students' learning has probably declined. For example, I cite the observation of Professor James Wandersee of Louisiana State University (LSU). Jim spent several summers working with my research team prior to his appointment at LSU. In one of our conversations, Jim commented that over a span of some twenty years, he and his teams had helped most of the school districts in the LSU area develop excellent activity-based science programs that had received local, regional, and national recognition. Within two years of the installation of NCLB programs in these districts, however, virtually all of these innovative programs had been wiped out.

When Barak Obama was elected president in 2008, I was hopeful that he might seek new leadership in the Department of Education that would be more understanding of what is needed to improve teaching and learning in public schools. Obama appointed Arne Duncan as Secretary of Education. He had been a successful superintendent of Chicago public schools, and a friend of the President. However, within a few weeks it was evident that Duncan was much more skilled at navigating the political waters of local school politics than in understanding how to help teachers optimize learning in their classrooms. While I applauded Obama's efforts to create a new national healthcare program, I did not see anything of value emerge for the improvement of education during his presidency.

We May Be at a Positive Turning Point in Education

In recent years, there have been remarkable efforts in schools from elementary schools to universities to move instruction away from students passively listening to lectures and memorizing information to pass typical true–false or multiple-choice exams. Instead, we are seeing movement toward instructional and evaluation activities that require learners to be much more engaged cognitively, socially, and as active participants in learning activities. While these activities vary widely in the details of their approaches, they all recognize that the central activity is to engage the students in the highest possible levels of meaningful learning. It has been gratifying to me to see that these new efforts are grounded in recent research in cognitive science, including some of the work done by my research teams over the years.

The recognition that college and university teaching can be improved if appropriate faculty training efforts were funded by the institution began to be more common in the 1990s. By this time the "cognitive psychology revolution" had largely replaced the useless behavioral psychology-based programs in faculty and student training centers that were established on most campuses. The explosive advances in personal computers, and the Internet, created many new instructional options, and both students and faculty needed help in mastering some of the new learning opportunities that were created.

The College of Agriculture and Life Sciences and the School of Veterinary Medicine at Cornell University were especially supportive of such training. I personally moved to spending about one-third of my time with this work in the 1990s. As noted earlier, Kathy Edmondson, one of my Ph.D. students, was hired to help in the Veterinary School in 1990, and she is still providing leadership as Assistant Dean of the College. The College is widely regarded as the world's premiere school of veterinary medicine in both research and teaching.

Today most colleges and universities have programs designed to help faculty gain an understanding of more recent research in cognitive psychology and the implications of this research for developing new instructional and evaluation strategies. Most of these programs rely extensively on the use of computers and the Internet. These centers have programs for both faculty and students. You can skim over the programs now available at Cornell University at: https://teaching.cornell.edu.

To learn more about what colleges and universities are doing to improve teaching and learning, I would suggest that you do a web search for your favorite schools using entries such as Center for the Improvement of Teaching and Learning at: _ (insert name of college or university).

The Growing Movement toward Research-based Innovation in College and University Teaching

In the sciences and mathematics, perhaps two book publications by the National Academy of Sciences (NAS)-National Research Council (NRC) were the most influential. One of these books, published in 1999, *How People Learn: Bridging Research and Practice*, presented some of the important research studies in cognitive psychology and their implications for teaching. A second volume published by the NAS-NRC in 2018, *How People Learn II: Learners, Contexts, and Cultures* further encouraged research-based innovations in college teaching. A pdf copy of both of these books can be downloaded at no cost at the NAS websites: https://doi.org/10.17226/9457 and https://doi.org/10.17226/24783.

From my perspective, both of these books suffer from a failure to present with great clarity the important differences between rote learning and meaningful learning. Neither book mentions Ausubel's Assimilation Theory of Learning or cites references showing successful instructional practices based on using his theory. They also fail to illustrate the role that constructivist epistemology plays understanding the concept and propositional nature of knowledge, and this is illustrated in Figure 5.5 of this book. With no linking words on lines connecting concepts in this figure, no propositions are formed, and the reader can only guess at what knowledge might be represented here. And incidentally, there are no figures in these books that a reader of this book would call a true concept map.

In spite of the limitations of the books cited above, they did cite important research by well recognized cognitive psychologists showing the importance of cognitive learning research to the improvement of science education. The books made a contribution to the growing recognition that college and university instruction must move toward strategies that encourage high levels of meaningful learning. The sheer distinguished reputation of the NAS-NRC in the eyes of scientists and mathematicians lent credibility to the messages of these books. The idea that new research

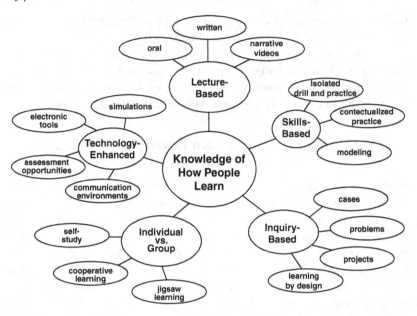

Figure 5.5   One of the diagrams presented in *How People Learn* (p. 18). With no linking words on the connecting lines to form propositions, one can only guess how these learning tools and approaches may be related.

in cognitive psychology pointed to the need for innovative instructional and evaluation practices was advanced by these books. Many of the later innovative efforts cited these books as part of the rationale for the new instructional methodologies.

The Growing Movement toward Active Learning Programs in College and University Science and Mathematics Instruction

In 2018, Joel Mintzes and Emily Walter recruited 125 authors to write sixty-one book chapters reporting on innovative active learning programs they conducted at their college or university. Eight distinguished scholars in the field of science education guided the project. The book was published by Springer Nature, Inc. in 2020 with the title: *Active Learning in College Science: The Case for Evidence-Based Practice.* Although the book presents primarily studies done in the sciences, many of the methods and strategies employed could also be applied to instruction in other fields.

The latter claim is well illustrated in chapter 30: "Active Learning Spaces: Matching Science Classrooms with Pedagogy," written by Jenay Robert et al. The authors describe two of the special rooms created at

Figure 5.6 An example of a classroom built at Penn State University specifically designed to facilitate active learning. The rooms have many electrical outlets and ample internet access jacks. Faculty from many different departments use such rooms.
(Photograph by Geffrey King of Pennsylvania State University.)

Pennsylvanian State University specifically designed to facilitate active learning. The administration at Penn State University has been strongly supporting a move toward active learning in all fields of study. They have provided faculty training opportunities to help older and younger faculty transition from traditional lecture–laboratory–discussion classes to classes where all students are engaged in small group activities and constructing progress reports on their learning. These reports are shared with other class members on white boards and white walls and with the use of digital projection when appropriate. Highly flexible learning spaces are needed, and the administration has supported the creation of such rooms. One example of these rooms is shown in Figure 5.6.

You will no doubt see the similarity of this room to the room shown earlier in this chapter as typical of the classrooms in John Dewey's Laboratory School. It is also similar in design and function to the room shown on the cover of our 1972 study report on exemplary science facilities shown in Chapter 4. One huge difference is that every learner now has access to the Internet, and potentially all the knowledge in the world. The professor's role is changed from dispensing information to helping students plan an effective study agenda and assisting them in their pursuit of the knowledge and understandings that are the substance of the course.

The authors build their case for moving toward active learning classrooms in part by citing research by Freeman and colleagues (2014). Freeman et al. conducted a rigorous meta-analysis of 225 studies in science that compared active learning with traditional lecturing. They cite the author's conclusion: The effect sizes in the meta-analysis were so large that the researchers were compelled to draw an analogy to medicine. That is, in medical trials, research is stopped when the new intervention is so superior that researchers cannot ethically justify continuing to enroll participants in the control conditions.

While it is probably true that the science and mathematics fields are leading the way in the use of active learning and concept mapping in colleges and universities, the same movement appears to be underway in other disciplines. For example, Collins and Nyenhuis (2020a) published a paper reporting positive results with the use of these strategies in political science. You can do a Google search on the use of these strategies in any field, and you are certain to find multiple entries.

So, the challenge is clear: hundreds of studies now show that moving instruction into reasonable forms of active learning and the use of concept mapping are not only justified but necessary if we are to give our students full value for their educational dollar and hours of effort.

In earlier chapters I discussed some of the work I did after I retired from Cornell University where we used concept maps effectively to better understand different domains of knowledge and to solve more quickly problems being addressed by the groups. In every case I worked on, the problems were addressed by a team of workers, not by individuals. It is not surprising that business consulting firms are now offering programs to help corporations adapt active learning strategies to solving corporate problems. One such firm is: Epignosis LLC, 315 Montgomery Street, 9th Floor, San Francisco, CA 94104, USA. Look at their website to see some of the training activities they offer to companies that are forward looking.

It should be obvious that students who have been engaged in active learning in some or most of their high school and college classes are going to be at a tremendous advantage in most future careers. Any college or university that is not providing such experiences for the majority of their classes is quite simply defrauding their students.

Taking Responsibility

From my perspective, the most promising outcome from student participation in good active learning programs may be the increased commitment to social responsibility that should accompany higher levels of meaningful learning and critical thinking. This is an issue I introduced earlier in this chapter, and I bring it up again because I believe active learning programs have much to offer to enhance the social responsibility of our students. At a minimum, I would expect to see a higher voting percentage for young people who had high-quality active learning experiences. I would also expect them to do better at discerning false claims, such as President Trump's claim in 2020 that 99 percent of positive test results for Covid-19 infection are totally harmless.

Throughout my career, I have seen the excitement that comes when the student who has been primarily memorizing information and understanding almost nothing suddenly discovers that they can learn meaningfully and understand and apply what they are learning. Some also express their anger that for so many years they have been deprived of the power of meaningful learning by poor education.

Laine Gurley was one of my Ph.D. students who continued teaching high school biology classes after her doctorate. She observed this transformation to committed learners in her students. She reported on her work in her 1982 Ph.D. thesis, "The Use of Gowin's Vee and Concept Mapping to Teach Responsibility for Learning in High School Biological Sciences." She credited the use of concept mapping and Gowin's Vee as important reasons why she observed this transformation in her students compared to other students in her high school. Gurley reported further on her work in *Concept Mapping: Learning How to Make Them, Use Them, and Teach Them to Others* (2014, self-published).

Good Education Should Lead to Higher Levels of Moral Development and Social Responsibility

During World War II, I was a preteen and later a teenager. I recall being horrified at some of the terrible things that were being done to war prisoners and to civilians in places such as Nazi Germany. And this was before we learned of the extermination of some 7 million Jewish people in Nazi death camps. I wondered then how anyone with a brain in their head could support what the Nazis were doing. I remember thinking at the time that the tragedies of fascism not only in Germany but also in Italy and Spain were at least partly the reason of a failure of the educational systems of those countries. The question for which I saw no answer at the time was: how can education be improved so that such terrible things never happen again. Religious institutions had been promulgating for centuries good teachings such as the Ten Commandments, but clearly something more was needed. In the USA and some other countries Neo-Nazi groups have been increasing in numbers and in their open disdain for Jews or other minority groups. In my view, schools cannot remain bystanders when it comes to issues of moral development and development of greater social responsibility.

Paulo Freire was one of the first to recognize that good education is the key to responsible citizenship. In his 1968 book, published in English in 1970 as *Pedagogy of the Oppressed*, he stressed that without education poor people will forever remain oppressed. He developed clever strategies to help poor Brazilians learn to read and write – and to become a powerful political force. Needless to say, Freire was not a popular person with the dictators of the time.

When I learned of Lawrence Kohlberg's (1984) work on moral development, I was intrigued. Kohlberg embraced Piaget's work on cognitive developmental changes in children. He applied similar reasoning in his studies of moral development in children. Upon closer analysis of Kohlberg's work, I saw the same shortcomings as in Piaget's work. His so-called distinct six stages of moral development appeared to me to be primarily artifacts of the research (Kohlberg, 1984). I was more impressed with Freire's idea that fraudulent education is disempowering and hence morally wrong. To me, the common school practice of students memorizing information to pass "objective tests" was a good example of fraudulent education.

While I see value in the work of Kohlberg and his followers in highlighting the importance of the affective domain in the design of educational programs, I do not see his work as part of a good foundation for building a comprehensive theory of education.

More recently there have been a number of scholars working to develop educational programs to enhance *social responsibility* of students. A good overview of this work can be found in Carbonero et al. (2017). Carbonero and his colleagues developed an educational program for secondary school students that involved their parents, their teachers, and of course their students. Their hypothesis was that: . . .*contextual variables, such as a child's willingness to accept social responsibility, also influence students' social and academic performance. Thus, students with greater responsibility have a better attitude toward their studies, resulting in higher academic achievement.*

The study was done over a two-year period, which I would regard as a reasonable time frame for such an endeavor. Students in early secondary school (ages 12–14) were enrolled in three middle-income urban schools.

One of the schools was selected at random to receive the experimental program. There were 132 students in the school with the experimental program and 139 students were in the two control schools.

The experimental program involved parents, students, and teachers with specially selected readings and activities based on the readings. Some of the activities involved specially trained tutors who helped focus individual and group efforts on issues of social responsibility. A variety of assessment measures were employed and most showed statistically significant differences favoring the students in the experimental school. The use of concept maps and Vee diagrams was not part of this program. Given the kinds of outcomes described in Gurley's book, cited earlier, it would be interesting to see the effect of these strategies on evidence of social responsibility.

Of course, there is always the question of the validity of the special evaluation tools used in this and similar studies. Were the special evaluation tools equally valid for both the experimental and the control students? By the very nature of the special traits the tests were designed to assess, there is an inevitable bias in favor of the students in the experimental program. Over the years there have been special programs introduced in schools to enhance student creativity, raise student IQ scores, advance student moral development, to increase student's racial tolerance and sensitivity, and the list goes on. Throughout this book I have argued that what we need are solid theory-based educational programs that seek to help everyone become competent in high levels of meaningful learning. To the extent that we succeed in this, all other good things will follow.

Hopeful Indicators for the Future

The growing movement toward active learning programs in all colleges and universities, as discussed above, is one promising new norm that is appearing. These programs will have the complementary benefit of teaching our students social responsibility. The educational programs that were so common during much of the time I was a student I characterize as: Memorize – Test – Forget. Such programs are inherently fraudulent, and therefore incapable of developing strong positive values and commitment in our students. I see hope in the emerging active learning programs and new curriculums that flow from these programs.

Let me illustrate this by citing the August 2019 issue of *The Science Teacher* that arrived as I was working on this chapter. This journal is the official journal of the NSTA, with over 50,000 members. The August issue was devoted to the topic of Earth and Human Activity. This issue opens with a guest special paper by Dr. Peter Raven, a highly respected biologist, and President Emeritus of the Missouri Botanical Garden. Peter points out that the world population was only about 1 million when agriculture was first invented 11,000 years ago. It has grown to about 7.7 billion people today. It is estimated that the population will be 11 billion people by the end of the century. Remember that children in our science classes today will only be in their 90s when this occurs, and of course their children and grandchildren will be much younger.

The food needed to feed 3 billion more people by 2100 is in itself a frightening statistic. But add to this problem the fact that oceans are rising, and billions of acres of land will be flooded by 2100. We already see chronic flooding and wind damage from increasing numbers and intensities of storms due to global warming. We know with certainty that rising levels of CO_2 are now the primary cause of global warming, but we face the frightening additional warming from melting glaciers and ice fields. Artic permafrost is thawing with the release of methane, whose greenhouse effects are worse than CO_2. Peter Raven goes on to describe some of the other threats we face for life on this beautiful planet.

This special issue of *The Science Teacher* continues with four papers reporting on classroom active learning programs dealing with the role of CO_2 in climate change, food shortages, community action programs and Red Tide issues. These are precisely the kind of instructional programs that are needed in our schools to prepare our students to be active, responsible adults committed to maintaining our planet.

Seek a Position in a School District That Supports Innovation

Not all school districts are committed to providing the best possible education for their children. James Gorman, a very able teacher I had been working with for several years, found that his school's support for the equipment and materials he needed to teach the kind of science he thought his students needed was steadily declining. Jim's students were enthusiastic about his classes, and he had to offer a special evening class to meet some of the demand. I advised Jim to relocate to a school that would offer him and his students the support they needed and deserved. Jim took a position at Mulpuk Regional High School, not far from his home. Jim had struggled to offer an engineering design course at his previous school, whereas Mulpuk was seeking to increase its offerings in this area and provided Jim with both the administrative and the financial support he needed.

In his previous school, Jim had designed a new course based on Dr. Charles Camarda's Innovative Conceptual Engineering Design (ICED) methodology. Charles is a NASA astronaut and Senior Advisor for Engineering Development at NASA, Langley Research Center. Charles provided the methodology and guidance to schools that sought to implement this program. Jim built this into a full-year course for high school students. The curriculum he designed employed key curriculum elements of "Epic" challenge: a student agency for ICED, a methodology that stresses the importance of failure, team cognitive diversity, mentors, low cost per student, and authentic audiences.[3]

A key feature of the course is that students work in teams to solve problems that they choose to address. These elements work together to establish a safe environment that encourages both *ingenuity*, the ability to cleverly solve difficult, real-world problems in an original way, and *creativity*, the ability to invent, in this case by designing and building prototypes. With these activities, Jim seeks to develop critical thinking research engineers who are ready to meet the next challenge and not just incrementally improve an existing design, but qualitatively improve the designs.

The ICED methodology stretches over the whole school year. During Quarter 1, the focus is on team learning and knowledge capture. Quarter 2 focuses on taking that learning and applying it to generate creative conceptual solutions to a real-world problem contained in the Epic challenge. One tangible outcome of this research is a poster to be presented at a symposium. Quarter 3 is spent in rapid concept development where they design, build, and test the prototypes. This often runs over into Quarter 4 of the school year where the students see their concepts mature and produce a final design report and a twenty-minute slide presentation. This presentation is usually given first at the high school and later at NASA Langley Research Center or at the Kennedy Space Center in May. Figure 5.7 shows three related posters developed by one of the research teams during Jim's 2018–2019 school year. In all, sixteen different posters were produced by the research teams. These posters have been mounted in one of the hallways of Mulpuk High School, and they draw attention from other students, parents, and visitors.

Jim Gorman and his students have made presentations of their work at regional and national conferences. I doubt if there are very many readers of this book who can look back on their high school science courses and say

---

[3] More information on the program is available at: https://docs.google.com/document/d/18uQHuGDxpKNTf_gBym4y58n6-oBJ_edMvh-ku4rCpRo/preview.

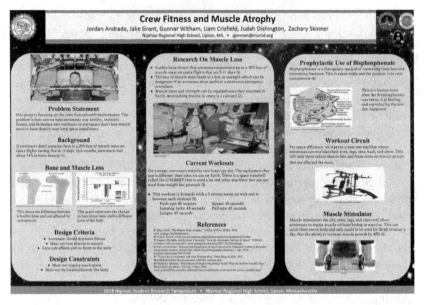

Figure 5.7   Three fitness posters produced by one of the teams in Jim Gorman's
class in 2018–2019.

that they were provided the valuable and exciting experiences Jim Gorman
and his students have achieved. It is my hope that this form and type of
course will become much more common not only in secondary school
sciences but in all curriculum areas.

New Hope for Improving Medical Education and Medical Practice

From various lines of evidence, we now know that the universe is about
14.5 billion years old, and that planet Earth was formed about 4.5 billion
years ago. As the Earth cooled, primitive forms of life appeared about
500,000 years ago and human-like life appeared about 100,000 years ago.
Until agriculture was invented about 20,000 years ago, finding adequate
food was the primary challenge faced by primitive people. As agricultural
practices improved, there was more time and more knowledge focused
on healthcare. Herbal medicine developed and much of it continues
today in some societies. It was not until the second half of the twentieth
century that chemical synthesis of medication became common. Research
on medical practices also became common and we experienced

enormous growth in medical specializations. The invention of computers and machines for diagnosing and treating medical problems greatly expanded. All this battery of changes helped to drive healthcare costs to approximately one-sixth of the US Gross Domestic Product, or some $800,000,000. And even at this level of funding, millions of Americans get limited healthcare at best. We must seriously address the question: how can we achieve better healthcare at lower cost? The short answer is through better education and better research.

My first encounter with failure in medical education was when I began dating my wife Joan in 1953. She was a student in medical technology and took most of the same courses taken by students planning to go on to medical school. Very few women went to medical school in those days. The University of Minnesota School of Medicine was internationally recognized both for teaching and for research. Many of Joan's classmates dated and later married men who became physicians. I found some of these men to be intelligent, deep thinkers, but some appeared to pass along by profusely memorizing information. It seemed obvious to me that the admission criteria being used by schools of medicine were failing to select the most qualified candidates and reject those who are potentially poor diagnosticians and poor in the practice of medicine.

My second encounter with medical incompetence occurred when our first son was born. Joan had been seeing the family doctor who had been her birth doctor. During the last month of her pregnancy, he advised that she did not need to see him unless she was feeling bad, and she did not. He never asked if she had any swelling in her legs – which she did, but she thought this must be normal. When she arrived at the hospital after her water broke, her doctor was surprised to see that she was in severe eclampsia and that she and the baby were too swollen for delivery. After thirty hours of contractions with no delivery, her doctor called in a competent gynecologist. Forty-eight hours after entering the hospital, son Joe was born with a three-inch lump on his head from pressure from Joan's pelvic bone pressed against his head. Fortunately, that subsided in a few weeks and son Joe turned out just fine. This event and many other encounters with medical incompetence motivated me to seek ways to improve medical education. I did not know at the time that more people die from medical malpractice than from automobile accidents in the United States. That fact is now well documented in multiple sources including any of the public search tools.

A significant part of my Ph.D. work focused on better ways to under-stand problem-solving abilities. I continued with this work, and I had published several papers on the subject. These papers attracted some attention from a few medical schools. My first invitation to consult with a medical school was in 1967. McMasters University Medical School in Hamilton, Ontario invited me to meet with their faculty. We discussed the problems created by excessive emphasis on memorizing information and too little emphasis on understanding the basic concepts and problem-solving strategies. I also introduced them to key ideas of Ausubel's Assimilation Theory of Learning. While many faculty generally agreed with my assessment of their problems, they saw no easy path to move away from the instructional and evaluation strategies they were currently using.

Although I continued to look for opportunities to work with medical education, it was not until 1982 that I received an invitation to lecture and do a workshop with faculty at Mercer University School of Medicine in Macon, Georgia. One of the professors, Mike Smith, had been following my work and used concept mapping and some of my ideas to improve his instruction. The faculty that attended my seminar were attentive and raised some good questions. In the end, there just was not enough support to move forward with significant curriculum changes and changes in instructional and evaluation strategies that would favor higher levels of meaningful learning.

Shortly after my work with Mercer University ended, I was approached by Professor Parker Small and Associate Dean Mauri Suter of the University of Florida Medical School in Gainesville, to help them transition to a medical curriculum that placed more emphasis on fundamental concepts of medicine and less emphasis on memorizing medical details. Both Parker and Dean were using concept mapping as a tool in their classes, and we were "all on the same page" with regard to needed curriculum and instructional changes. I made several visits to Gainesville, and I was beginning to think we might begin to build a model program for medical education. Unfortunately, both Parker and Dean took sabbatical leaves about this time. Shortly after they returned from the sabbatical leave, they both decided to take early retirement. Without their leadership there simply was no way to go forward with the program we had been planning. Once again, what appeared to be a promising effort to create a model medical education program fell by the wayside.

I had three pleasant visits with Dean Elizabeth Armstrong, the Associate Dean for Instructional Innovation at Harvard Medical School, a well-received seminar and workshop with faculty at the School of Osteopathic Medicine at the Philadelphia College of Osteopathic Medicine, and a number of exchanges of emails and phone calls with faculty and administration at other medical schools. None of the latter contacts led to a sustained collaborative effort to improve medical education.

As noted earlier in this chapter, Professor Gowin and I were successful in helping to transform programs at the College of Veterinary Medicine at Cornell University, and those programs continue to be models for veterinary medicine all over the world. Kathy Edmondson, who I mentioned earlier in this chapter, continues to provide training in concept mapping and instructional design in the College. She also chairs the section on Medical Education for the American Educational Research Association (AERA). In a recent visit with Kathy, she described some of the good innovative research on teaching that has been reported in her AERA section meetings.

Another of our Cornell Ph.D. students who studied with me, Barbara Daley, specialized in nursing and adult education, and she played a key role in bringing about the current widespread use of ideas of meaningful learning and the use of concept mapping in nursing education. Barbara and two of her colleagues, Sarah Morgan and Sarah Beman Black, published a review of her work and the work of others presented in a review of research done on the effectiveness of concept mapping in nursing education (Daley, Morgan, and Beman Black, 2016).

In a recent email, Barbara wrote:

> I noted in the book (Novak, 2018) your comment on how resistant medical education was to changing how they teach. This was so very true for a very long time. Both nursing and medical education resisted implementing most anything from education. You will be happy to know, however, that this is starting to change, and I am encouraged by the interest I now see in concept mapping in medical education as well as nursing education. It is very different than a few years ago. The accreditation criteria in medical education changed, and that led to a big push to use research-based education strategies in medical education, concept maps being one. I am very pleased the article: https://www.mededpublish.org/manuscripts/380 on concept mapping in medical education that physician colleagues and I did now has over 15,000 views. That is the most views of any of their articles since the journal was initiated.
>
> As to medical education, I guess I am hopeful, because I did a visiting professorship with the Uniformed Services University of the Health Sciences Hula (USUHS) in Bethesda, MD in 2016. They are the University that prepares physicians, nurses and dentists for the military and they were starting a Health Professions Education (HPE) program to prepare mostly physicians to be educators. The HPE program is located in

the medical school, and they have been most interested in concept maps and including them in the HPE program so future physician educators can use them. Specifically, the folks that teach clinical reasoning see great value in the maps.

In a recent conversation with Barbara, she reiterated her optimism that medical education is definitely moving in the direction of teaching and evaluation that places emphasis on meaningful learning with team-based problem-solving becoming the standard practice in many medical schools. Concept mapping is also becoming a standard tool in many of these programs. One example of this at the University of Algiers was reported by Darian Nasser (2018). Table 5.1 shows that students in this study were highly positive about the value of concept maps in learning to assess risk factors in cardiovascular disease. I find it gratifying to see the extent to which medical schools are moving toward an emphasis on meaningful learning using concept maps to facilitate team problem-solving with real-world cases. I also take some satisfaction that most of these study reports provide one or more references to our research work.

Team-based learning is definitely becoming more popular in the health sciences (see Leupen, 2020). It is also gaining popularity for instruction in many fields as indicated earlier.

Table 5.1 *Learner's responses about concept maps through problem-based learning used in understanding risk factors (RF) for cardiovascular disease (CVD) (% agree/disagree)*

No	Statements	SD	D	N	A	SA
1	Concept map was a meaningful learning tool to facilitate lifelong knowledge	0	0	2.5	10	87.5
2	Helped to integrate basic and new knowledge	0	0	2.5	20	75
3	Helped to link RF for CVD theoretical information to estimate risk level using FRS tool	0	0	2.5	15	80
4	Helped to solve problems in RF for CVD using FRS diagnostic	0	0	2.5	10	87.5
5	Would you continue to use concept map to solve problems in RF for CVD using FRS diagnostic	0	0	2.5	7.5	90

Recording from learner's responses: SD strongly disagree, D disagree, N neutral, A agree, SA strongly agree, The answers were recorded on a typical five-level Likert scale (1 = strongly disagree, 2 = disagree, 3 = neither agree nor disagree, 4 = agree and 5 = strongly agree).

Helping People Deal with Climate Change and Associated Physical and Social Changes

Currently the five-day weather forecast you receive is about 90 percent accurate. Forecasts for hurricane strengths and pathways have a similar high degree of accuracy. Most people rely on these forecasts and take actions accordingly. Climate change forecasts are based on the same sciences as weather and hurricane forecasts. However, only about 70 percent of the US population recognizes that climate changes are occurring, and this could have terrible consequences for the future. The problem is that storm effects from hurricanes on a target region can be seen in two or three weeks, whereas the effects from climate change will appear much more slowly and it will be decades if not centuries before the worst events occur. So, for the near-term, climate change is seen by many as an *inconvenient truth*, to use the title of Alan Gore's 2006 documentary. This popular view is that, well maybe this will happen, but why worry about it now? Tragically, they fail to see that climate change is already having dire consequences as evidenced by record high global temperatures year after year, record-setting forest fires in some regions of the world, and rising sea levels everywhere. Fortunately, the majority of world leaders are being rational about the problem and are taking steps to attempt some mitigation of the problem.

Climate scientists have established with a high level of certainty that the primary cause of global warming has been the increase in so-called greenhouse gases. Carbon dioxide is the primary culprit in this category, but methane gas is also a significant contributor to global warming. These gases deter heat radiation from leaving the earth leading in time to atmospheric heating and global warming. Siberia and the Arctic have huge amounts of methane gas trapped in their vast tundra fields. With relatively small amounts of further global warming, these gases could be released relatively quickly, producing a sudden uptick in global greenhouse gas levels.

The primary source of carbon dioxide comes from the burning of fossil fuels including coal, petroleum, and natural gas. For more than 100 years, motor vehicles have been the primary consumers of fossil fuels and producers of carbon dioxide. There is clear evidence that this situation is about to change. In a recent report published in *Science*, the authors report:

> The signs of vehicle electrification are growing. By 2025, Norway aims to have 100% of its cars be either an electric or plug-in hybrid unit, and the Netherlands plans to ban all gasoline and diesel car sales by the same year. By 2030, Germany plans to ban internal combustion engines, and by 2040,

France and Great Britain aim to end their gasoline and diesel car sales. The most aggressive electric vehicle targets are those set by China, which has almost half the global electric vehicle stock and where 1.1 million electric vehicles were sold in 2018. Europe and the United States each have just over 20% of the global stock, with electric car sales of 380,000 and 375,000 units, respectively, in 2018. (Crabtree, 2019)

Other more recent reports have been even more optimistic about the shift to electric vehicles. Some go so far as to predict that the only place to buy gasoline-powered cars by 2050 will be in a used car lot. Judging from what has happened to stock for Tesla Corporation in 2020, a company that makes only electric-powered vehicles, the markets appear to be predicting a very bright future for these vehicles. Tesla is also expanding enormously its production of solar panels.

What Will Happen if Most Vehicles Become Self-driving?

For reasons given above, it is highly likely that most vehicles will be electric powered by the middle of the twenty-first century. It is also likely that new models of the vehicles will have increased driver assistance electronics. Currently there is considerable debate as to the relative safety of human versus autonomous driven cars. Statistics show autonomously driven cars do relatively well on divided highways, but they have more difficulty with congested city streets. My experience with Uber and Lyft is that their GPS can get me close to the building of my destination, but either I or the driver must often intervene to get me to the door of my destination. Given the rate of technological advance in the past thirty years, and the huge economic advantage of driverless cars, buses, and trucks, it is highly likely that we shall see predominantly driverless vehicles by mid-century. When this occurs, the predictions are that most city dwellers will no longer own cars or have two-car garages. It is hard to imagine what kind of changes will take place in cities and in the countryside when most cars, passenger vans, and trucks are autonomously driven. Can you imagine what will happen to the millions of people now employed as car, bus, or truck drivers? This is the kind of social upheaval our schools must prepare our students to manage.

At this time, the options for people transport are an automobile or a bus. While it is true innovations such as those introduced by Lyft and Uber provide other passenger option, they are still one vehicle with one driver and one to three passengers. There is some use of autonomously driven vans, but most of these are experimental at this time. So far as I can find on the Internet, none of these has advanced to widespread use anywhere in the world. This is almost certain to change in the next five years. I think we shall see a huge increase in various kinds of autonomously driven electric vans. Also, during the next few decades, we will see a huge rise in electric-powered vehicles of all types.

A special report by a commission chaired by Professor Crabtree (2019) discussed the problems associated with changes we can expect with the transition to electric vehicles and increased use of solar energy. Published in the world's most read scientific journal, *Science*, below are a few paragraphs from that report.

> Currently, the major deterrent to more rapidly expanding use of electric automobiles and trucks are the costs and limitations of lithium battery technology. Lithium batteries are not only relatively expensive, the world supply of lithium is limited. Unfortunately, China controls much of the world supply, and this speaks to their determination to move all future automobiles to electric powered vehicles. Even with the current state of battery technology, it is probable that we shall see not only worldwide rapid expansion of electric vehicles but also rapidly increased use of solar power for residential and commercial purposes. (Crabtree, 2019)

The report also commented that advances in solid-state electrolytes increase the safety associated with the lithium-ion battery thermal runaway reaction phenomenon that causes batteries to burst into flames if their temperature exceeds about 150°C. The report in *Science* continues:

> There is now an intense drive to develop lithium metal anodes and solid-state electrolytes spanning academic, government, and industrial laboratories. Toyota announced its intention to have batteries with lithium anodes and solid-state electrolytes ready for electric vehicles by the early 2020s. (Crabtree, 2019)

If we pause for a moment to consider what happened in the area of information storage and processing, we see the possibility of parallel development happen in the field of electrical energy production and storage. The first transistors could replace the vacuum tubes in radios and other electronic equipment. We went from devices much smaller than the radio to devices that were orders of magnitude smaller than vacuum tubes but capable of storing and processing vastly more information than tube-based technology. Consider for a moment all the information storage and processing capabilities of your cell phone. It is almost inevitable that something similar to this revolutionary transformation will occur in the field of electrical energy production and storage. Moreover, this is likely to occur in a few decades rather than a few lifetimes. It will occur in the lifetime of schoolchildren now in our classes. Are we preparing them to deal with this changing world?

There is an inexhaustible supply of solar energy available to us from the sun. However, even if new technologies allow us to produce and store solar energy at almost no cost, there is still the problem of providing energy for ocean vessels, airplanes, and long-haul trucks. At least for the foreseeable future, we will need to find methods of offsetting carbon dioxide production from these sources. We will need to find more effective, creative solutions to atmospheric carbon dioxide reduction than current methods such as planting trees and growing algae. A strong international organization focused on problems of CO_2 reduction may be a temporary solution, but this is not going to be sufficient to achieve the level of CO_2 reduction that will be needed to reach pre-industrial levels of greenhouse gases.

We shall require massive improvements in our educational systems throughout the world to deal with the massive problems brought on by climate change. I believe that the progress we have made in our education research programs over the past half-century can contribute significantly to the educational changes that will be needed in the next half-century to help solve these problems and can be achieved with valid theory-based research and new educational practices.

Climate change is a problem we must begin to deal with immediately. However, there is no quick solution for this problem. It will be with us for generations to come. For this reason, I am pleased to have the continuing cooperation of two former Cornell University Ph.D. students, Jane Heinze Fry and her husband Gene Fry who have provided selected references dealing with climate change and these are given in Appendix 2. Furthermore, they provide contact information for individuals who would like to receive assistance from them in the future.

What May We Learn from the Covid-19 Flu Pandemic?

The Spanish Flu, the last pandemic to strike planet Earth, occurred during 1918 to 1919. It was estimated that some 500 million people in the world contracted the disease. The number of deaths from the virus was estimated at 17 million to 50 million (Wikipedia, 2020). Initially it was believed to be caused by a bacterium. It was not until the 1930s after more was learned about the existence of viruses that these were identified as the cause of flu. The first vaccine for the flu was administered in1945. In subsequent years it was established that avoiding crowds and using face masks were helpful to limit the spread of influenza. We also learned that the influenza virus easily mutates, and new strains of the virus require that new vaccines must be developed continuously. As of this writing new variants of Covid-19 are arising, and we don't know when this process will end.

Our grandson works for a company where he managers energy supplies for numerous customers. Except for occasional training programs at company headquarters, he has done all of his work from home, and very little changed when the virus struck. Our son works for the Limited Corporation, managing store design for Bath and Body stores. He moved some of his equipment and drafting table to his home and now works successfully from there. The coronavirus has forced many companies to explore opportunities created by high-speed internet services, and I expect much of this activity will continue with thousands of corporations after the pandemic is over. There will always be a need for team problem-solving sessions of the kind described in this book. However, these may occur only one day per week, with the remaining time used to do more creative work in preparation for the next meeting. I would not be surprised to see concept mapping play an important role in this kind of creative work. Concept maps would also be very helpful in video team conferencing using software such as Zoom.

We are witnessing a significant increase in consumer online purchasing of everything from daily meals and groceries to every kind of consumer goods including automobiles. My wife and I live in a "locked down" facility for seniors. We are learning various ways to order online the relatively few things we need from day to day. My one complaint about online shopping is that I have age-related vision problems, and the young people who design websites do not appreciate how small fonts in pastel colors are very difficult to work with for many older people, and also for a significant percentage of the total population. I keep telling my ophthalmologists that I have trouble reading their cards. They politely agree that this is a problem, but so far none have changed the color or font size used on them. This can be even more aggravating with cell phones and business websites.

Challenging as Covid-19 is for homemakers and businesses, the problems schools and colleges are facing are perhaps even greater. This may not be the case for the very small percentage of schools that already have been operating primarily via the Internet. However, this is not the case for the vast majority of schools and colleges. Many inner-city schools are also facing the challenge of the need to continue to provide meals for their students who were dependent on free or subsidized meal programs. In some areas, the schools were also providing meals to adults in low-income areas.

Unlike many businesses, most teachers and most schools are not prepared to offer extensive online instructional programs, nor are their students experienced in using such instruction. Millions of students have taken Khan Academy online courses and similar courses offered by some colleges, but even so, these represent a small minority of the total student enrollments. If school lockdowns continue into the 2021–2022 academic year, most schools will need to explore ways to do more online teaching, guidance, and counseling. New alternatives for providing meals and other needed services will need to be developed.

Currently some 20 percent of workers are unemployed, and with state and local agencies that tally these figures struggling with incompetent data systems to manage unemployment, the real numbers may be substantially higher. Even as the numbers stand now, they are significantly higher than the unemployment rate during the Great Depression of 1929–1932. Under the leadership of Franklin Roosevelt, the United States saw the creation of the Works Projects Administration (WPA) in 1935, the Rural Electrification Act (REA) in 1936, and the Civilian Conservation Corps in 1937. All of these agencies provided badly needed jobs and badly needed improvements to the nation's infrastructure. Today we need massive improvements to the nation's highways, bridges, airports, and high-speed internet services almost everywhere. Doing all of these things would provide many good jobs. Moreover, with long-term bond interest rates now near zero percent, there is no rational reason why all of these things could not be done – other than the lack of leadership. Perhaps before this book is published, we may see the needed leadership come forward.

On the world scene, especially the southern hemisphere, the situation is even more dire than for the United States. In a March 2020 publication, the World Bank wrote:

> We are living amidst what is potentially one of the greatest threats in our lifetime to global education, a gigantic educational crisis. As of March 28, 2020, the COVID-19 pandemic is causing more than 1.6 billion children and youth to be out of school in 161 countries. This is close to 80% of the world's enrolled students. We were already experiencing a global learning crisis, as many students were in school but were not learning the fundamental skills needed for life. The World Bank's "Learning Poverty"

indicator – the % of children who cannot read and understand at age 10 – stood at 53% of children in low- and middle-income countries – before the outbreak started. This pandemic has the potential to worsen these outcomes even more if we do not act fast.[4]

The authors go on to discuss the importance of good food and nutrition programs as a necessity for good student learning. With the necessity of social distancing, schools and cities will need to be creative in finding new ways to operate and support school and community meal programs. With unemployment rates running 20 percent or higher in many of the needy communities, there should be ways to redesign meal programs to meet nutritional needs during this pandemic – and to provide much needed jobs to teenagers and adults in these communities.

It is also imperative that every community find ways to make modern technology and the Internet available to every child and adult to facilitate their learning. In the United States, we need something like the 1936 Rural Electrification Act. We need a national Everyone Connected to High Speed Internet Act, that includes programs to train teachers and businesses in best ways to use the Internet more effectively. We saw how a little of such training had remarkable results in Panama.

Finally, I believe we need a national program to help students, parents, and teachers understand the important differences that occur when learners are learning at high levels of meaningful learning, as contrasted with learning primarily by rote memorization. We need to help them understand the concept and propositional nature of knowledge and the processes by which new knowledge is created. We need to encourage the use of instructional practices such as active learning programs where the students can actually create new knowledge, individually or as a small group. They need to understand that good knowledge is something we need to share with the world. Unlike food or most things, there is no limit to how widely we can share new knowledge. Knowledge and caring for others are two things we can share without limit. To the extent we help to do this, we help to make this a better world for everyone. What I am proposing is too important to be lodged in the Department of Education with its poor track record for improving school learning. An organization similar to the Environmental Protection Agency may be needed. Maybe something like an Agency for Creation and Distribution of New Knowledge is needed?

---

[4] "Educational Challenges and Opportunities of the Coronavirus (COVID-19) Pandemic," March 30, 2020, Worldbank.org. https://blogs.worldbank.org/education/educational-challenges-and-opportunities-covid-19-pandemic.

Initially, I had planned to include revamping of the United States Health Care System as one of the worthy goals we should pursue as we work our way out of the Covid-19 Pandemic. But as I began to write on this subject, every proposal I tried to devise simply would face too many obstacles. I believe the other proposals I have made are viable, and if they succeed over time, they will establish the groundwork for a new and better healthcare system. This system would also be much more cost effective, since it would engage a better-educated, and better-informed public in partnership with medical professionals who now struggle with too many patients who are woefully ignorant and often badly misinformed. They would also have the support of more voters who believe in the science behind medicine and will be better voters when it comes to healthcare issues. I am convinced that we now know enough about how to help people learn that a national program committed to this goal, and with the proper leadership, would be the best investment we can make as we work to recover from the Covid-19 pandemic.

The Journey Forward

We began in the 1950s to search for a better theory of knowledge and to seek a better theory of learning than those that were popular at that time. The behavioral psychology that dominated the literature in the 1950s and 1960s failed totally to address problems associated with human learning such as methods to enhance human problem-solving success. Moreover, behavioral psychology was rooted in positivist epistemology that dominated much of western thinking in the 1950s. Our research group was one of the first to embrace the view of knowledge as rooted in evolving conceptual schemes as put forth by James Conant in 1948. An example of major conceptual change in biology occurred in 1953 when Watson and Crick published a paper describing the structure of DNA, the genetic material that regulates everything in organisms from microbes to man (see Watson, 1968). My research group embraced the Assimilation Theory of Learning that David Ausubel first put forward in 1962. Although our views were unpopular at the time, by the late 1980s cognitive psychology and constructivist epistemology had become the dominant views, ideas we had been helping to develop. These views began to move education away from traditional lecture – memorize – test – forget educational programs toward the emerging collaborative teams of active learning instructional programs that are becoming popular today.

Perhaps the most important single advance resulting from our research program was the invention of the concept map knowledge representation tool in the early 1970s. The tool was initially devised to show explicitly changes in children's concept and propositional knowledge as they proceeded through carefully designed A-T lessons in science. We subsequently found that concept maps could be used to represent knowledge in a highly concise manner in any discipline and with almost any age group.

The highly creative work of Dr. Alberto Cañas and his team at IHMC led to the creation of CmapTools, a software suite that made the creation and use of concept maps much easier. It also provided the additional capability of incorporating any digital material as part of a concept map's digital file. This feature facilitates the use of concept maps for organizing and archiving expert knowledge. Concept maps are now being used in educational and research programs of every kind throughout the world.

In Chapter 4, I presented evolving patterns we observed in school instructional programs, room furnishings, use of audiovisual aids, and student–staff relations. These evolving patterns all point in the direction of what we are observing today in classrooms that are engaged in the best active learning instructional programs. Increasingly, we are observing similar patterns emerging in many workplace settings. Given the half-century history of these evolving patterns, we can implement the best practices suggested with confidence that we are moving in the right direction.

In Chapter 3, I described the efforts made by my students and I to create a viable theory of education. We sought to put forward a theory based upon a cognitive theory of learning, a constructivist epistemology, and a viable theory of curriculum and instruction. The theory sought to integrate the five elements involved in education: teacher, learner, curriculum, social context, and evaluation, with the primary goal of enhancing meaningful learning. Cornell University Press published my first effort – *A Theory of Education* – in 1977. Following two and then three decades of applying this theory in various educational and occupational settings, Routledge published, in 1998 and 2010, two updated versions of my theory together with new illustrative examples. This book is probably my final effort to promulgate my theory of education, and to illustrate how it can be applied to help people learn.

In this chapter I have chosen to focus on what I believe is the greatest challenge to civilization, namely climate change. Global nuclear war could also wipe out civilization as we know it, but so far world leaders have kept such an event in check. Improving education is also the best deterrent to nuclear war.

The last time most of the northern hemisphere was covered with ice was about 20,000 years ago when the atmosphere began to warm, and the ice caps receded close to where they are today. However, after the industrial revolution began around 1750, population growth began to accelerate along with the burning of fossil fuels, and we began to observe significant increases in global atmospheric temperatures. It took scientists a while to establish that this rise in atmospheric temperatures was caused primarily by increases in carbon dioxide levels. Carbon dioxide in the atmosphere acts as a screen that retards heat radiation from leaving the earth. Now we know with a high degree of certainty that we must not only drastically reduce adding more carbon dioxide to the atmosphere but also find ways to remove much of what man and forest fires have put there. If we fail to do this, the horrible environmental problems that will ensue could lead to global political problems and possibly global nuclear war with life-destroying nuclear winter.

We have only one rational pathway forward and that will require helping all the people of the world become committed meaningful learners, dedicated to a worldwide effort to save and preserve planet Earth. The educational programs that will be needed to achieve this goal are the same as those that are needed to make life on Earth more civilized, more humane, and happier for everyone. I hope the peoples of the world will find the wisdom, the energy, and the motivation to save planet Earth as we know it – and ourselves.

Testing My Theory of Education

One Method of Testing My Theory of Education

Any valid theory should be testable. I have presented positive results for a number of educational innovations that were consistent with my theory of education or showed educational or creative productions resulting from our work that supported the theory. However, these were mostly real-world cases that involve multiple variables, as is usually the case when dealing with real-world problems. Here I wish to propose a relatively simple test of my theory that could be done by anyone with access to thirty or more subjects aged 18 or older. The study might be titled: How (insert label for the group) Think About the World.

Follow these steps:

Introduce them to my Learning Approach Questionnaire (see below). You might say you are interested to learn how your _____ sample of people thinks about the nature of knowledge and how they learn. We have generally found all groups we have worked with to be quite willing to do the questionnaire seriously.

I have suggested some questions to add below the questionnaire. These are biographic indicators that you can correlate with the subject's test score. You may want to add a question or two of your own.

THE QUESTIONNAIRE – Biographical

How many years of your education were in schools that were:

Public _____ Charter _____ Private_____ Religious_____

How would you rate the quality of your education?
    Did you vote in the last:

    Local election _____ State election _____ National election _____?
    Did you vote: Independent__ Republican__ Democrat __Other__
    Name of Respondent _____
    You may want to include additional questions of your own.
    Any comments on the questionnaire?

    _____
    _____
    _____
    _____

Most groups should be able to complete the questionnaire in 15–20 minutes. If time allows, you may want to get some oral feedback from individuals in your group. In this case, it is wise if you can record the comments and add the name of the person.

The Questionnaire

Learning Approach Questionnaire

(Make copies for each participant)
    Different people have different styles and approaches to learning. The purpose of this questionnaire is to assess what type of learning approach you most typically use. Please choose one of the following options for your response to each item. Your comments about any statement are also appreciated.

    SD means you strongly disagree with the statement
    D means you disagree with the statement
    U means you are undecided and neither agree nor disagree with the statement
    A means you agree with the statement
    SA means you strongly agree with the statement

1. I generally put a lot of effort into trying to understand things which initially seem obscure.
    SD   D   U   A   SA
    Comments:

2. I find it better to have a fairly good grasp of the main ideas of a topic and build up my knowledge of the details based on those main ideas.
SD D U A SA
Comments:

3. I find it is usually best to memorize a great deal of what I have to learn.
SD D U A SA
Comments:

4. While I am studying, I often think of real-life situations to which the material I am learning would be useful.
SD D U A SA
Comments:

5. One of the most important considerations in choosing a course is whether or not I will be able to get a good grade in it.
SD D U A SA
Comments:

6. I try to relate new material as I am reading it to what I already know on the topic.
SD D U A SA
Comments:

7. I often find myself questioning things I hear in lectures or read in books.
SD D U A SA
Comments:

8. In trying to understand new topics, I explain them to myself in ways that make the most sense to me.
SD D U A SA
Comments:

9. I find it useful to get an overview of a new topic for myself, by seeing how the ideas fit together.
SD D U A SA
Comments:

10. I prefer presentation of the simple truth uncomplicated by controversial ideas or alternative explanations.
SD D U A SA
Comments:

11. I realize that "truth" is forever changing as knowledge is increasing and feel comfortable with this.
SD D U A SA
Comments:

12. The best way for me to really understand what technical terms mean is to remember the textbook definitions.
     SD   D   U   A   SA
     Comments:

13. I learn most things by rote, going over and over them until I know them by heart.
     SD   D   U   A   SA
     Comments:

14. I believe strongly that one aim in my life is to discover my own philosophy and belief system and to act in accordance with it.
     SD   D   U   A   SA
     Comments:

15. I spend a lot of my free time finding out more about interesting topics which may be at best only indirectly related to my classes.
     SD   D   U   A   SA
     Comments:

16. Although I generally remember facts and details, I find it difficult to fit them into an overall view of the subject.
     SD   D   U   A   SA
     Comments:

17. My studies have modified my views about such things as politics, my religion, and my philosophy of life.
     SD   D   U   A   SA
     Comments:

Scoring the Questionnaire

The questionnaire was designed to assess the degree to which the testee seeks to achieve high levels of meaningful learning. These items were written so that Strongly Agree (SA) is the best indicator of this and should score 5 points, Agree (A) scores 4 points, Undecided (U) score 3 points, Disagree (D) scores 2 points, and Strongly Disagree (SD) answers should score 1 point.

   Items: 1, 2, 4, 6, 7, 8, 9, 11, 14, 15, and 17 score 5 points for Strongly Agree: (SA).
   Items: 3, 5, 10, 12, 13, and 16: score 5 for Strongly Disagree: (SD).

Thus, maximum positive score is: 85; minimum score is 17.

Rationale of the Study

As noted in Chapter 3, five elements are involved in any educational experience:

1. The learner, 2. The teacher, 3. The subject matter. 4. The context for the learning, and 5. The evaluation of the learning.

Each of these elements should be designed to promote meaningful learning. When this is accomplished at a high level, we should observe:

> ## A Theory of Education
>
> **Meaningful learning underlies the constructive integration of thinking, feeling, and acting leading to empowerment for commitment and responsibility.**
> **J. Novak**

Hypothesized results:

1. Most groups will show a wide range of scores on the questionnaire.
2. Subjects with the highest scores will have the highest voting records, especially for local elections.
3. Type of school attended will have little effect on test score.
4. Number of years in each type of school will have little effect on scores.
5. I would be interested in the average scores of those who vote: Democrat, Independent, or Republican.
6. Comments made by students should tend to match "objective test score."
7. If you choose to interview some or all of the students in your study, statements should generally be in line with the choices they made on the objective test.
8. You might want to compare scores for positions of subjects taken on current "hot button" issues, e.g., should sales of assault rifles be banned?

    If you do your own study to test my theory, I would very much appreciate hearing from you: jnovak@ihmc.us (Preferred) or jdn2@cornell.edu.

Special Resources on Climate Change

As this is written, the world is suffering with the worst pandemic in a century. Although effective vaccines are now available, global access to them is still not ensured, and so the death toll will continue to rise. It is too soon to predict the total loss of life and even more difficult to predict what will happen to the economies of the world. What we know for certain is that the death toll will be the highest we have seen in a century, and the economic losses will be in the many trillions of dollars. Some significant portion of these deaths and economic losses are the result of being too slow at applying the science that was known. In the United States, there were often mixed messages on the importance of wearing masks and maintaining social distance between individuals. Too often political or economic concerns took precedence over the science resulting in successive outbreaks around the United States. We shall never know the exact extent to which President Trump's questioning of the science and offering known invalid solutions contributed to the loss of life in the United States. We do know at this time that only a handful of developed countries currently demonstrate higher fatality percentages per capita than the United States.

We are in the early stages of a much greater tragedy facing the peoples of the world, namely climate change. There were, of course, massive climate changes in the first 4 billion years of the Earth's history. The fossil record shows that humans have been around for only about 100,000 years. Moreover, human beings produced relatively little carbon dioxide until manufacturing took off 250 years ago and then when automobiles became commonplace less than 100 years ago. The explosive growth in the number of human beings on Earth, combined with the growing demand for energy from coal, natural gas, and oil, is the reason we are experiencing the rapid change in our climate. We have the highest carbon dioxide levels in 14 million years. Not surprisingly, we already suffer the hottest temperatures in over 100,000 years, with three to eight times as much heating to come should we not take action.

As noted in Chapter 5, Jane Heinze-Fry and her husband, Gene Fry, have offered to assist readers of this book in building their understanding of the problems of climate change. They have prepared the materials given below as a starting point for anyone interested in the subject. They also have provided contact information for individuals who wish to communicate directly with them. Jane and Gene will be around long after I have passed. I am pleased to have their offer of continuing support in this effort.

Gene and Jane Heinze-Fry have made available to readers of this book special resources that they have developed to help educators and the general public better understand the enormous problems that face civilizations on planet Earth. Climate change has been occurring on planet Earth for all of its 4.5 billion years of existence. The difference is that the *rate* of climate change has increased dramatically such that changes that occurred in a century are now occurring in a decade. It is now well established that most of this climate change has been caused by a dramatic increase in the amount of carbon-containing gases being released into the atmosphere by humans, and further exacerbated by loss of forests, ice sheets, glaciers, and snow.

Gene and Jane Heinze-Fry are retired educator-researchers who now devote full-time to help achieve public understanding of the magnitude of the problems brought on by climate change. They work to enlist others' help to prevent large sections of our planet from becoming uninhabitable with attendant crop failures and mass starvation. I am pleased to make some of their work available to the public via this book and via the many resources they place within easy access.

Gene and Jane have prepared the material that follows.

In Our Opinion: The Case for Meaningful Learning

Gene Fry, Ph.D. and Jane Heinze-Fry, Ph.D.

As a species, we have proved that we can expand our populations throughout the world and claim much of Earth's ecosystems for ourselves. (Since 1970, biomass of wild mammals has fallen 82 percent or more, as it has, more broadly, for vertebrates [60 percent].) There is much to celebrate in this human expansion, with increases in standards of living and reductions in poverty for many. As our population expands, however, we have not proved that we leave the Earth in as good condition for succeeding generations as we inherited from prior generations. That is particularly true at this point in time. Never has it been more important to learn about how our world works and to do the right thing with that knowledge.

The largest challenge humans have ever faced is the current rapid climate change. The climate system is complex. Climate change has multiple causes. It has multiple effects. The two primary causes are adding huge amounts of carbon to the air and decreasing how much sunlight Earth reflects, such as by melting ice and snow. Without strong measures to decarbonize our energy systems and remove most carbon we have put into the air, key impacts of climate change follow.

1. Hotter temperatures, with humidity, will make it too hot for humans to work or even survive, in far more times and places on Earth.
2. Widespread crop failures from heat, drought, and flooding will cut food supplies in half.
3. Rising seas put a good bit of Earth's property value under water all or part of the year.
4. Available fresh water declines steeply, as evaporation intensifies and glaciers disappear.
5. Stronger hurricanes and storms pound coastal and some interior populations.
6. Wildfires destroy many or most forests, further limiting CO_2 capture and oxygen production.
7. Billions of people migrate, and conflicts escalate.
8. The sixth great extinction on planet Earth in the last half billion years will occur!

Again, to prevent or reduce all of these horrors, not only must we stop adding carbon to the air, we must remove most of what we have already added as soon as we can.

Why is understanding and responding to climate change so challenging? It is complex. Complexity is increased by the presence of feedbacks and delays between the causes and their impacts. Social, economic, and political factors establish a complex playing field of ideas. These complexities challenge our abilities to understand both the nature of the problem and the best solutions to the problem.

What we know is that the scale of the human response must match the scale of the problem. The work that must be done is to make decisions and take appropriate collaborative action at the community, state, nation, and global levels. We can survive as a species if we learn to both mitigate and adapt to these challenges.

Gene and Jane have provided below additional reference materials especially selected for readers of this book:

Climate Change: Causes, Impacts, Solutions

https://cmapspublic2.ihmc.us/rid=1QFJ88YMG-M7FBBS-5N06/
Climate%20Change%20Bite-Sized2.cmap

Global Warming - So What?

www.globalwarming-sowhat.com/

A good starting point to learn about current climate change is the Special Climate double issue of *Time*, September 23, 2019: *2050: The Fight for Earth*. These notes support the claims made by Gene Fry and Jane Heinze-Fry.

Impacts
1. Heat
   The Hottest City on Earth, p. 28.
2. Crops
   Wine-growing, p. 55; Lithuania crop failures, p. 55; California Central Valley, p. 61.
3. Floods
   Flooding West Africa, p. 47; *Mississippi River Delta and US East Coast*, p. 61; flooding in Guyana damages GDP, land displacement, p. 94.
4. Drought, Agriculture, Energy Production
   Glacial melt, p. 47; drought in Mexico City, p. 61; loss of glacier surface area in Peruvian Andes impact agriculture and hydropower, p. 75; Patagonian ice fields melting at fast rate, p. 75; ice sheets in Antarctica shrinking, exacerbating melting glaciers, p. 90.
5. Landslides from Flash Flooding
   Africa's coastline, p. 47; US Midwest, p. 61; flash flooding and landslides common in South America's northwest coast, p. 75.
6. Fires
   Higher temp increases risk of fires in boreal forests, p. 55; deforested tropical lands (mostly Brazilian Amazon) emit carbon second only to China and US.

7. Droughts and Migration

Sahel, p. 47; droughts in Honduras, El Salvador, Guatemala, Nicaragua contribute to migration to Mexico and US, land displacement forcing migration, p. 94.

8. Food Web and Fisheries

Drop in fisheries, p. 47; reduced plankton affecting marine food chain in North Sea, p. 55; *Preserving Ocean Life Is Essential to Preserving Human Life*, p. 66; krill populations shrink as ice habitat melts, undercutting Antarctica's food web.

Solutions

1. Energy Innovation

Africa Can Be the Launchpad for a Green-Energy Revolution, p. 40.

2. Carbon Sequestration

The Great Green Wall of Africa, p. 44; *Take a Walk on the Rewilding Side*, p. 52.

3. Policy; Investment

The Climate Caucuses, p. 59; *Our Cities Cannot Become Climate Sanctuaries for the Rich*, p. 88; The pension fund trying to change the world, Hiromichi Mizuno taking the long view by valuing environmental, social, and governance characteristics of investments.

4. Optimism

How We Survived Climate Change, p. 14, emphasis on spread of youth activism; *The Women Who Will Save the World*, p. 42; Greta Thunberg, p. 48; The devastation of climate change is real. But there are reasons to be hopeful, p. 50. Inserts by optimists are sprinkled through this issue.

5. Complexity: Feedbacks

Hot temperature causes permafrost to melt and increases wildfire risk in Siberia, p. 55; also, northern Alaska melting of Arctic permafrost, releasing more carbon dioxide into the air, creating a vicious climate (reinforcing) feedback loop, p. 61.

6. The Call to Learn and Do

Preserving ocean life is essential to preserving human life, p. 66.

"We increasingly understand how little we actually know, and in these precarious times, it is essential that we have a firm grasp on whether we can afford to add new stressors to the ocean's ecosystem."

Gene Fry and Jane Heinze-Fry
Jane Heinze-Fry;
E-mail: jahfry@rcn.com
Gene Fry;
E-mail: gene.fry@rcn.com

References

Achterberg, C. L., Novak, J. D., and Gillespie, A. H. 1985. "Theory-Driven Research as a Means to Improve Nutrition Education." *Journal of Nutrition Education*, 17(5), 179–184.

Al-Kunifed, A., and Wandersee, J. H. 1990. "One Hundred References Related to Concept Mapping." *Journal of Research in Science Teaching*, 27(10), 1069–1075.

Anderson, J. R. 1983. *The Architecture of Cognition*. Cambridge, MA: Harvard.

Ausubel, David P. 1962. "A Subsumption Theory of Meaningful Verbal Learning and Retention." *Journal of General Psychology*, 66, 213–224.

——— 1963. *The Psychology of Meaningful Verbal Learning*. New York: Grune and Stratton.

——— 1968. *Educational Psychology: A Cognitive View*. New York: Holt, Rinehart and Winston.

——— 2000. *The Assimilation and Retention of Knowledge: A Cognitive View*. Dordrecht/Boston/London: Kluwer Academic Publishers.

Ausubel, David P., Novak, Joseph D., and Hanesian, Helen. 1978. *Educational Psychology: A Cognitive View*, 2nd ed. New York: Holt, Rinehart and Winston. Reprinted, 1986, New York: Werbel & Peck.

Bartlet, Frederick C. 1932. *Remembering*. Cambridge: Cambridge University Press.

Belluck, P. "To Really Learn, Quit Studying and Take a Test." *New York Times*. Jan. 20, 2011, www.nytimes.com/2011/01/21/science/21memory.html.

Bowen, B. L. 1972. "A Proposed Theoretical Model Using the Work of Thomas Kuhn, David Ausubel and Mauritz Johnson as a Basis for Curriculum and Instruction Decisions in Science Education." Unpublished doctoral thesis, Cornell University.

Bretz, S. 1994. "Learning Strategies and Their Influence Upon Students' Conceptions of Science Literacy and Meaningful Learning: The Case of a College Chemistry Course for Non-Science Majors." Unpublished doctoral thesis, Cornell University.

Bretz, S. L. and Meinwald, J. 2001. "The Language of Chemistry." *Journal of College Science Teaching*, 21, 220–224.

Brewer, A., Helfgott, M. A., Novak, J. D., and Schanhals, R. 2012. "An Application of Cmaps in the Description of Clinical Information Structure and Logic." *Global Advances in Health and Medicine*.

Cañas, Alberto J., Ford, Kenneth M., Novak, Joseph D., Hayes, Patrick, Reichherzer, Thomas R., and Suri, Niranjan. 2001. "Online Concept Maps: Enhancing Collaborative Learning by Using Technology with Concept Maps." *The Science Teacher*, 68(4), 49–51.

Cañas, A. J., and Novak, J. D. 2008. "Concept Mapping using CmapTools to Enhance Meaningful Learning." In A. Osaka, S. B. Shum, and T. Sherborne (eds.), *Knowledge Cartography: Software Tools and Mapping Techniques* (pp. 25–46). London: Springer.

Carbonero, M. A., Carbonero, L. J., Lourdes Otero, M.-A., and Monsalvo, E. 2017. "Program to Promote Personal and Social Responsibility in the Secondary Classroom." *Frontiers in Psychology*, 8, 809. Published online May 22. doi: 10.3389/fpsyg.2017.00809.

Chi, M. T. H., and Koeske, R. 1983. "Network Representation of a Child's Dinosaur Knowledge." *Developmental Psychology*, 19, 1, 29–39.

Collins, B., and Nyenhuis, R. 2020a. "The Effectiveness of Concept Maps for Students' Learning and Retention." *Journal of Political Science Education*. DOI: 10.1080/15512169.2020.1775090.

Collins, B., and Nyenhuis, R. 2020b. "Active Learning in Political Science." In Joel J. Mintzes and Emily M. Walter (eds.), *Active Learning in College Science: The Case for Evidence-Based Practice (pp. 3–12)*. New York: Springer.

Conant, J. B. 1947. *On Understanding Science: An Historical Approach*. New Haven, CT: Yale University Press.

Crabtree, G. 2019. "The Coming Electric Vehicle Transformation." *Science*, 366 (6464), 422–424.

Daley, B. J., During, S. J., Torre, D. M. 2016. "Using Concept Maps to Create Meaningful Learning in Medical Education." *MedEdPublish*. www .mededpublish.org/manuscripts/380/.

Daley, B. J., Morgan, S., and Black, S. B., 2016. "Concept Maps in Nursing Education: A Historical Literature Review and Research Directions." *Journal of Nursing Education*, 66(11), 611–639. Also at: https://pubmed.ncbi.nlm .nih.gov/27783817/.

Darwin, C. 1873. *The Origin of Species by Means of Natural Selection*. New York: Hurst and Company.

Donaldson, M. C. 1978. *Children's Minds*. New York: Norton.

Dunn, B. R., Novak, J. D., Hill, R., MacQueen, K., and Wagner, L. 1989. "The Measurement of Knowledge Integration using EEG Frequency Analysis." Paper presented at the 1989 annual meeting of the American Educational Research Association, San Francisco, California.

Edmondson, K. M. 2004. "Assessing Science Understanding through Concept Maps." In J. J. Mintzes, J. H. Wandersee, and J. D. Novak (eds.), *Assessing Science Understanding: A Human Constructivist View* (pp. 15–40). San Diego, CA: Academic Press.

Edmondson, K. M., and Novak, J. D. 1993. "The Interplay of Scientific Epistemological Views, Learning Strategies, and Attitudes of College Students." *Journal of Research in Science Teaching*, 32(6), 547–559.

Flat Earth Believers: "Modern Flat Earth Beliefs." https://en.wikipedia.org/wiki/Modern_flat_Earth_societies.

Ford, K. M., Canas, A. J., Jones, J. C., Stahl, H., Novak, J. D., and Adams-Webber, J. 1991. "ICONKAT: An Integrated Constructivist Knowledge Acquisition Tool." *Knowledge Acquisition*, 3, 215–236.

Fraser, K. 1993. "Theory Based Use of Concept Mapping in Organizational Development: Creating Shared Understanding as a Basis for the Cooperative Design of Work Changes and Changes in Working Relationships." Ph.D. Dissertation, Cornell University.

Fraser, Kym, and Novak, Joseph D. 1998. "Managing the Empowerment of Employees to Address Issues of Inter-Employee Cooperation, Communication, and Work Redesign." *The Learning Organization*, 5(2), 109–119.

Freeman, S., Eddya, Sarah L., McDonough, M., Smith, Michelle K., Okoroafor, N., Jordt, H., and Wenderoth, Mary P. 2014. "Active Learning Increases Student Performance in Science, Engineering, and Mathematics." *Proceedings of the National Academy of Sciences of the USA*, 111(23), 8410–8415. doi: 10.1073/pnas.1319030111.

Frisendal, Thomas, 2012. "Design Thinking Business Analysis: Business Concept Mapping Applied (Management for Professionals)," New York, Springer. Frisendal.

———. 2016. *Graph Data Modeling for NoSQL and SQL: Visualize Structure and Meaning*. Basking Ridge, NJ: *Technics Publications*.

Gurley-Dilger, L. I. 1982. "Use of Gowin's Vee and Concept Mapping Strategies to Teach Responsibility for Learning in High School Biological Sciences." Unpublished Ph.D. thesis, Cornell University.

Gurley, L. 2014. *Concept Mapping: Learning How to Make Them, Use Them, and Teach Them to Others*. Self-published book.

Hagerman, Howard. 1966. "An Analysis of Learning and Retention in College Students and the Common Goldfish (*Carassius auratus*, Lin)." Ph.D. thesis, Purdue University.

Heinze-Fry, Jane A., and Novak, Joseph D. 1990. "Concept Mapping Brings Long-Term Movement Toward Meaningful Learning." *Science Education*, 74(4), 461–472.

Helm, Hugh, and Novak, Joseph D. (eds.) 1983. *Proceedings of the International Seminar on Misconceptions in Science and Mathematics Conference, June 1983*. Ithaca, NY: Cornell University, Department of Education.

Hibbard, K. M., and Novak, J. D. 1975. "Audio-Tutorial Elementary School Science Instruction as a Method for Studying of Children's Concept Learning: Particular Nature of Matter." *Science Education*, 59(4), 559–570.

Hilgard E. R. 1948. *Theories of Learning*. New York: Appleton-Century-Crofts.

Hoffman, B. 1962. *The Tyranny of Testing*. New York: Crowell-Collier Press.

Hoffman, R. R., Coffey, J. W., Ford, K. M., and Carnot, M. J. 2001. "STORM-LK: A Human-Centered Knowledge Model for Weather Forecasting." In *Proceedings of the 45th Annual Meeting of the Human Factors and Ergonomics Society*. Santa Monica, CA: HFES.

Hoffman, R. R., Coffey, J. W., Ford, K. M. and Novak, J. D. 2006. "A Method for Eliciting, Preserving, and Sharing the Knowledge of Forecasters." *Weather and Forecasting*, 21, 416–428.

Johnson, Mauritz, Jr. 1967. "Definitions and Models in Curriculum Theory." *Educational Theory*, 17(2), 127–140.

Karpicke, J. D., and Blunt, J. R. 2011. "Retrieval Practice Produces More Learning Than Elaborative Studying with Concept Mapping." *Science*, 331 (6018), 772–775. doi:10.1126/science.1199327.

Kohlberg, L. 1984. *Essays on Moral Development, Vol. II: The Psychology of Moral Development: The Nature and Validity of Moral Stages*. San Francisco: Harper & Row.

Kuhn, David J. 1967. "A Study of Varying Modes of Topical Presentation in Elementary College Biology to Determine the Effect of Advance Organizers in Knowledge." Ph.D. thesis, Purdue University.

Kuhn, D. 2000. "Metacognitive Development." *Current Developments in Cognitive Science*, 9, 178–181.

Kuhn, T. S. 1962. *The Structure of Scientific Revolutions*. Chicago, IL: University of Chicago Press.

Kulik, James A., Kulik, Chen-Lin C., and Cohen, Peter A. 1979. "Research on Audio-Tutorial Instruction: A Meta-Analysis of Comparative Studies." *Research in Higher, Education*, 11(4), 321–341. http://hdl.handle.net/2027 .42/43586.

Leupen, Sarah. 2020. "Team-Based Learning in STEM and the Health Sciences." In Mintzes, Joel J. and Walter, Emily M. *Active Learning in College Science. The Case for Evidence-Based Practice* (pp. 219–232). New York: Springer.

Macnamara, John. 1982. *Names for Things: A Study of Human Learning*. Cambridge, MA: MIT Press.

Mali, Ganesh B. (1979). Development of Earth and Gravity Concepts among Nepali Children, *Science Education*, 63(5), 685–691.

Marton, Ference and Söljö, R. 1976a. "On Qualitative Differences in Learning, 1: Outcome and Process." *British Journal of Education Psychology*, 46, 4–11.

Marton, Ference and Söljö, R. 1976b. "On Qualitative Differences in Learning, 2: Outcomes as a Function of Learners Conception of the Task." *British Journal of Educational Psychology*, 46, 115–127.

Mintzes, J. J., Cañas, A., Coffey, J., Gorman, J., Gurley, L. Hoffman, et al. 2011. "Comment on 'Retrieval Practice Produces More Learning than Elaborative Studying with Concept Mapping.'" *Science* 334(6055), reply 453.

Mintzes, Joel J., and Walter, Emily M., 2020. *Active Learning in College Science: The Case for Evidence-Based Practice*. New York: Springer.

Mintzes, J. J., Wandersee, J. H., and Novak, J. D. (eds.) 2004. *Assessing Science Understanding: A Human Constructivist View*. San Diego, CA: Academic Press.

Mintzes, J. J., Wandersee, J. H., and Novak, J. D. (eds.) 2005. *Teaching Science for Understanding: A Human Constructivist View*. New York: Academic Press.

Misconceptions in Science and Mathematics: 1983–1995. The Proceedings of these conferences can be obtained at: www.mlrg.org.

Moon, B. M., Hoffman, R. R., Novak, J. D., and Cañas, J. J. 2011. *Applied Concept Mapping: Capturing, Analyzing, and Organizing Knowledge.* New York: CRC Press.

Molnar, Alex. 1994. "Education for Profit: A Yellow Brick Road to Nowhere." *Educational Leadership*, 52(1), 66–71.

Nasser, Darian. 2018. "Using Concept Mapping through Problem-Based Learning to Facilitate Lifelong Knowledge of Risk Factors for Cardiovascular Diseases: Case University of Algiers." Paper presented at the PBL 2018 International Conference, PBL for the Next Generation: Blending Active Learning, Technology and Social Justice, Santa Clara, California, Feb. 16–19.

National Academy of Sciences National Research Council. 1999. *How People Learn: Bridging Research and Practice.* Washington, DC: The National Academies Press. https://doi.org/10.17226/9457.

National Academies of Sciences, Engineering, and Medicine. 2018. *How People Learn II: Learners, Contexts, and Cultures.* Washington, DC: The National Academies Press. https://doi.org/10.17226/24783.

National Research Council (NRC). 1996. *National Science Education Standards.* Washington, DC: National Academy Press.

Neisser, Ulric. 1967. *Cognitive Psychology.* New York: Appleton-Century-Crofts.

Nesbit, J. C. Nesbit, and Olusola, O. A. 2006. "Learning with Concept and Knowledge Maps: A Meta-Analysis." *Review of Educational Research*, 76(3), 413–448.

Nonaka, I., and Takeuchi, H. 1995. *The Knowledge-Creating Company.* Oxford: Oxford University Press.

Novak, J. D. 1958. "An Experimental Comparison of a Conventional and a Project Centered Method of Teaching a College General Botany Course." *Journal of Experimental Education*, 26, 217–223.

1961. "An Approach to the Interpretation and Measurement of Problem-Solving Ability." *Science Education*, 45, 122–131.

Novak, J. D. 1963. What should we teach in biology? *NABT News and Views*, 7(2), 1. Repr. in *Journal of Research in Science Teaching*, 1(3), 241–243.

1964. "Importance of Conceptual Schemes for Science Teaching." *The Science Teacher*, 31(6), 10.

Novak, J. D. 1971. "A Study of Cognitive Subsumption in the Life Sciences." *Science Education*, 55(3), 309–320.

1972a. "Facilities for Secondary School Science Teaching." *The Science Teacher*, 39(3), 2–13.

1972b. *Facilities for Secondary Science Teaching: Evolving Patterns in Facilities and Programs.* Washington, DC: National Science Teachers Association.

1973. "Evolving Patterns in Secondary School Science Facilities." *The American Biology Teacher*, 35(6), 319–321.

1977a. *A Theory of Education.* Ithaca, NY: Cornell University Press; paperback, 1986. Spanish, Madrid: Alianza Editorial; Portuguese, Lisboa: Platano; Basque, 1996, Zarautz (Gipuzkoa).

1977b. "An Alternative to Piagetian Psychology for Science and Mathematics Education." *Science Education*, 61(4), 453–477.

1983. "Human Constructivism: A Unification of Psychological and Epistemological Phenomena in Meaning Making." *International Journal of Personal Construct Psychology*, 6, 167–193.

1993. "Human Constructivism: A Unification of Psychological and Epistemological Phenomena in Meaning Making." *International Journal of Personal Construct Psychology*, 6, 167–193.

1998. *Learning, Creating, and Using Knowledge: Concept Maps as Facilitative Tools in Schools and Corporations*. Mahwah, NJ: Lawrence Erlbaum & Associates. Spanish, 1998, Madrid: Alianza Editorial. Portuguese, 2000, Lisboa: Platano Edicoes Tecnicas. Italian, 2001, Trento: Edizioni Erickson. Finnish, 2003, Jyuvaskyla, Finland: PS-kustannus.

2002a. "Meaningful Learning: The Essential Factor for Conceptual Change in Limited or Appropriate Propositional Hierarchies (LIPHs) Leading to Empowerment of Learners." *Science Education*, 86(4), 548–571.

2002b. "Using Concept Maps to Facilitate Classroom and Distance Learning." *Scuola & Citta*, 2, 112–114.

Novak, J. D. (2003). A Preliminary Statement on Research in Science Education. *Journal of Research and Science Teaching*, 40(1), pS1–S7.

Novak. J. D. 2004. "Reflections on a Half Century of Thinking in Science Education and Research: Implications from a Twelve-Year Longitudinal Study of Children's Learning." *Canadian Journal of Science, Mathematics, and Technology Education*, 4(1), 23–41.

2010. *Learning, Creating, and Using Knowledge: Concept Maps as Facilitative Tools in Schools and Corporations*, 2nd ed. New York: Routledge, Taylor-Francis. Italian translation: Erickson, 2012.

2011. "A Theory of Education: Meaningful Learning Underlies the Constructive Integration of Thinking, Feeling, and Acting Leading to Empowerment for Commitment and Responsibility." *Aprendizagem Significativa em Revista / Meaningful Learning Review*, 1(2), 1–14.

Novak, J. D., and Cañas, A. J. 2004. "Building on New Constructivist Ideas and the CMapTools to Create New Model for Education." Closing Lecture. First International Conference on Concept Mapping: Theory, Methodology, Technology. Pamplona, Spain. University of Navarra.

2006. "The Origins of the Concept Mapping Tool and the Continuing Evolution of the Tool." *Information Visualization Journal*, 5(3), 175.

Novak, J. D., and Cañas, A. J. 2007. "Theoretical Origins of Concept Maps: How to Construct Them and Uses in Education." *Reflecting Education*, 3(1), 29–42. www.reflectingeducation.net/index.php/reflecting.

Novak, J. D., and Gowin, D. B. 1984. *Learning How to Learn*. New York and Cambridge: Cambridge University Press. (Also published in eight other languages.)

Novak, J. D., and Iuli, R. I. 1995. "Meaningful Learning as the Foundation for Constructivist Epistemology." In F. Finley, D. Allchin, D. Rhees, and

S. Fifield (eds.), *Proceedings of the Third International History, Philosophy and Science Teaching Conference*, Vol. II. Minneapolis, MN: University of Minnesota.

Novak, J. D., and Musonda, D. 1991. "A Twelve-Year Longitudinal Study of Science Concept Learning." *American Educational Research Journal,* 28(1), 117–153.

Novak, J. D., Meister, M., Knox, W. W., and Sullivan, D. W. 1966. *The World of Science Series.* Books One to Six. Indianapolis, IN: Bobbs-Merrill Company, Inc.

Novak, Joseph D., Donald G. Ring, and Pinchas Tamir. 1971. "Interpretation of Research Findings in Terms of Ausubel's Theory and Implications for Science Education." *Science Education,* 55(4), 438–526.

Novak, J. D., and Symington, David. 1982. "Concept Mapping for Curriculum Development." *V.I.E.R. (The Victorian Institute of Educational Research),* 48, 3–11.

Nussbaum, J., and Novak, J. D. 1976. "An Assessment of Children's Concepts of Earth Utilizing Structured Interviews." *Science Education,* 60(4), 535–550.

Palmer, Cristi. 1996. "In Vitro and In Vivo Effects of Bicarbonate on Botrytus Cinceria." Unpublished Ph.D. thesis, Cornell University.

Popper, K. R. 1959. *The Logic of Scientific Discovery.* New York: Basic Books. 1982. *Un-ended Quest: An Intellectual Autobiography.* London: Open Court.

Postlethwait, S. N., Novak, J. D., and Murray, H. T., Jr. 1969. *The Audio-Tutorial Approach to Learning through Independent Study and Integrated Experience,* 2nd ed. Minneapolis, MN: Burgess.

Postlethwait, S. N., Novak, Joseph D., and Murray, H. T., Jr. 1972. *The Audio-Tutorial Approach to Learning,* 3rd ed. Minneapolis, MN: Burgess.

Ravitch, D. 2010. *The Death and Life of the Great American School System.* n.p.: Capitol Reader and Shamrock New Media.

Rowe, Mary B. 1974. "Wait-Time and Rewards as Instructional Variables: Their Influence on Learning, Logic, and Fate Control. I. Wait-time." *Journal of Research in Science Teaching,* 2(2), 81–94.

Schneps, M., and Sadler, P. (1989). *Private Universe Project.* Cambridge, MA: Harvard-Smithsonian Center for Astrophysics, Science 6–8, 9–12.

Schwab, J. J. 1973. "The Practical 3: Translation into Curriculum." *School Review,* 81(4), 501–522.

Senge, P. M. 1990. *The Fifth Discipline: The Art and Practice of the Learning Organization.* New York: Doubleday.

Silesky, O. 2008. "Concept Maps and Standardized Tests." PowerPoint presentation, Sept. 23, Tallinn, Estonia.

Skinner, B. F. 1938. *The Behavior of Organisms: An Experimental Analysis.* New York: Appleton-Century-Crofts.

Symington, D., and Novak, J. D. 1982. "Teaching Children How to Learn." *The Educational Magazine* 39(5), 13–16 (Australian).

Torre, D., Daley, Barbara J., Picho, K., and Durning, Steven J. 2017. "Group Concept Mapping: An Approach to Explore Group Knowledge

Organization and Collaborative Learning in Senior Medical Students."
Medical Teacher 39(10), 1051–1056. doi: 10.1080/0142159X.2017
.1342030.

Toulmin, S. 1972. Human Understanding. *Vol. I:* The Collective Use and
Evolution. Oxford: Oxford University Press.

Tyler, R. W. 1977. "Foreword." In J. D. Novak, *A Theory of Education* (pp. 7–8).
Ithaca, NY: Cornell University Press.

Underwood, Emily, 2015. "Expanding our Mental Maps." *Science*, 352, 1378.

von Glasersfeld, E. 1984. "An Introduction to Radical Constructivism." In P.
Watzlanick (ed.), *The Invented Reality* (pp. 17–40). New York: Norton.

Vygotsky, L. S. 1962. *Thought and Language* (trans. and ed. Eugenia Hanfmann
and Gertrude Vakar). Cambridge, MA: The MIT Press.

1986. *Thought and Language* (trans. and ed. Alex Kozulin). Cambridge, MA:
The MIT Press.

Waterman, Robert H. 1995. *What America Does Right*. New York: Penguin,
Plume.

Watson, J. D. 1968. *The Double Helix: A Personal Account of the Discovery of the
Structure of DNA*. New Haven, CT: Yale University Press.

Whorf, B. L. 1956. *Language, Thought and Reality: Selected Writings of Benjamin
Lee Whorf* (ed. and with an introduction by John B. Carroll). Cambridge,
MA: The MIT Press.

Index

CPSIA information can be obtained
at www.ICGtesting.com
Printed in the USA
LVHW051924210722
723963LV00006B/114